T0162611

REVIVAL
UNLIMITED
FROM THE SHOULDER

PAUL JUBY

Inspiring Voices®

Inspiring Voices books may be ordered through booksellers or by contacting:

Inspiring Voices
1663 Liberty Drive
Bloomington, IN 47403
www.inspiringvoices.com
1 (866) 697-5313

Because of the dynamic nature of the Internet, any web addresses or links contained in this book may have changed since publication and may no longer be valid. The views expressed in this work are solely those of the author and do not necessarily reflect the views of the publisher, and the publisher hereby disclaims any responsibility for them.

Any people depicted in stock imagery provided by Thinkstock are models, and such images are being used for illustrative purposes only. Certain stock imagery © Thinkstock.

ISBN: 978-1-4624-1066-8 (sc)
ISBN: 978-1-4624-1067-5 (e)

Library of Congress Control Number: 2014920100

Printed in the United States of America.

Inspiring Voices rev. date: 11/18/2014

This book is dedicated to Michael and Janet Moorthy

FOREWORD

"Revival Unlimited" has over 150 poems written in a very positive Christian way. They are "wake-up calls" to non-Christians, fence sitters and "comfortable" Christians. Also a positive reminder to active Christians and Pastors and to their churches that without enthusiasm little can be done. That enthusiasm to fish for souls must continue all the time, not just periodically..

This book is similar to "Revival Hallelujah" in that it is written "from the shoulder".. For some, including clergy it is not altogether met with approval. The poems point out weaknesses in churches and this finger pointing does not go down well with a few.. We have to face facts, no church is 100% perfect and most are far below such a standard. What is mostly lacking is spiritual enthusiasm.

Every poem has been written with positive solutions and written prayerfuuly. The aim is to bring members alive, to interest our non-believing friends. The whole purpose is to bring Revival to any and every Church. To bring evangelism in as a permanent part of each church in the truest of Biblical ways.

Truly dedicated prayer-filled Churches will find the miracle of spiritual snowballing – meaning that such churches will receive many blessings and see Revival as a wonderful fact.

This is a call to admit and act upon the fact that there is much to be done, and through the Lord Revival will be accomplished.

CONTENTS

ALL AMATEUR

Call us amateur Christians !
Ninety nine per cent of us.
Serving God,
Not counting the cost.
Following Jesus,
Following His disciples.
Never a thought for rewards.
Serving God,
No strings attached.
Why is this so ?
Because love rules,
Service ruled by love,
Nothing more.
We strive hard,
Our tasks with one aim
Following our Lord Jesus Christ.
The disciples were our example,
They put service above all.

They lived in terrible times,
Eventually, sadly,
Almost all lost their lives.
These days there is much less risk,
Even so,
We must be prepared.
Jesus showed love supreme,
Hung on a cross
For each of us..
Amateur Christians ?
We must prove our worth,
Dedicating our whole lives,
Happy to serve.
There is no retirement
And love continues
Right to our final days.
Hallelujah !

ALL SORTS

It's wonderful !
Christ's Church.
It has all sorts.
Every language,
Every colour,
Every nation,
All equal in God's sight.
The young and the old,
The illiterate,
The learned,
The jobless,
The rich and the poor.
All sorts.
God's gates -
They are always open.
All invited.
There are no barriers,
Christ is for all.

And yet,
Most people do not enter.
We who believe,
We must give our lives,
Go to the unsaved,
Show them the way,
That they are all loved,
They are all welcome.
We cannot sit back,
We are duty bound
To meet all sorts.
Jesus always met the people,
All sorts.
So must we.
Show your worth
Go out to serve
And rejoice at the task.
Hallelujah !

"AMEN" WITH HOES

All who are believers pray.
Some stay close to Jesus
While others drift away.
They pray,
They think He does not answer
So they ask and ask and ask.
They have no deep faith.
Their prayers are robotic,
They need to start afresh.
Someone said,
God expects you to use a hoe,
To use it after the Amen!"
It makes sense.
Too often prayers are just words.
Selfish words.

Do not presume,
Do not leave all to God.
Belong to God's Team
And use that hoe.
You'll find more answers.
Prayers become alive.
Godly team work.
It's you and God together.
Sitting back is useless,
Bring your faith to the front
And enter a new prayer world.
Just remember,
Use that hoe,
Hallelujah !

AT ALL COSTS

When Jesus preached
He did not count the cost.
He was bold and fearless,
Yet he new He would suffer,
Knew He would be killed.
He gave His life for love,
The love of God for us.
Are we in any way prepared ?
Prepared to serve at any cost ?
Prepared to face opposition ?
Prepared to put Jesus first ?
If you truly believe
Then do not count the cost.
Be certain,
Jesus rules !
Jesus comes first,

Ahead of our families
And ahead of all else.
Nothing must block the way
Nothing interfere,
Nothing clash.
Jesus died for us,
We must be dedicated,
Be complete Christians.
Loyal, steadfast, faithful,
There are no options.
Take up your cross
Follow Him !
Never, never hang back.
Eternal life will be yours,
Rely on that !
Hallelujah !

BALL IS IN YOUR COURT

Have you ever been spoon fed ?
Someone holding your hand ?
Someone telling you what to do ?
Someone looking after you ?
Even though you have grown up !
Stand on your own feet !
Learn to be independent.
Work out your life
Like the king or a queen
of a kingdom !
Then whatever you do
The ball is in your court.
You make the decisions,
That is common-sense.
Just one thing left out !
So far it's all you,

But who made you ?
Where are you with God ?
Think a lot on this.
Open your Bible,
Read John 3 verse 16.
Ponder a few minutes
Ponder longer.
Go to Matthew Chapter 5,
The sermon on the mount
And think very hard !
Then you decide !
Decide to follow Christ.
You take those steps,
The ball is in your court,
It's for you with Jesus
Hallelujah !

BE AMAZED !

Remember this,
Never, never take life for granted.
From this day
To your very last day,
Be amazed !
From the day you found Jesus
Be amazed !
Stay amazed !
You found great love,
You found a great helper,
You found a great friend.
You received happiness,
You received a new life
So be truly amazed !
Let God's words stir you.
The Christmas story,
The way Jesus preached,

The miracles,
His care and concern,
Then the Easter story.
Be amazed !
Then think of yourself,
He chose even you !
He knew you by name,
He knows your strengths,
Your weaknesses,
And He chose you !
What for ?
To save lives,
To bring more to know Him.
Respond in full,
Stay thoroughly amazed,
And thank |Him.
Hallelujah !

BE A BROTHER LAWRENCE

There was a simple monk,
Brother Lawrence was his name.
He was a great Prayer Warrior.
His duties were lowly,
Scrubbing floors,
Cleaning pots and pans
Yet he was special,
Soaked in prayer.
He used his days well,
He talked to Jesus.
Some could not tell,
Could not tell
When he was not praying.
He worked very hard,
He prayed while he worked,
Living with Jesus.

Too many of us,
We spend only minutes
Talking to Jesus.
Just minutes in prayer.
Mostly empty praying.
Valueless praying.
We should be ashamed !
Learn to pray while working,
Pray as you walk.
Pray every hour,
Even just in short ways.
Live with Jesus,
Live with Him all day long.
Be a Brother Lawrence,
Have God-filled days.
Hallelujah !

BE A FANATIC !

It's an unpopular name
Being a fanatic !
Most are fierce,
Could be evil,
Most are rebels.
Hold on though !
Be a gentle fanatic.
Be a loving fanatic,
Be different for Jesus.
Stand out !
Oppose the secular advance,
Speak out !
Rebel against drink and drugs,
Against greed,
Against every wrong doing.
Be courageous !

Do it the Jesus way.
Sadly many churches fail,
Many Christians fail
To show what Jesus taught.
We must share Jesus,
We must evangelise,
We must save lives,
We must stir others,
Others to catch on fire.
Gently,
Lovingly,
Firmly,
Courageously.
Go for it !
Go for Jesus !
Hallelujah !

BE DIFFERENT !

There is a saying,
Comes from Norfolk County.
"Do Different".
It means stand out !
Too many follow the crowd,
It's the easiest way.
Easy to be ordinary,
Easy to accept the secular,
Easy to be accepted.
It's the wrong way !
Far better,
Far, far better
To be different.
Different for Jesus.
Why so ?
Why stand out ?
Why be unpopular ?

Purely, simply
There is only one way,
The Jesus Way.
He died for you,
He loves you by name.
He will guide you,
He'll be your friend
Always and forever.
Be different,
Full of faith,
Full of enthusiasm,
Full of happiness.
Aim to help others,
To show others Jesus,
Aim to teach,
Teach the Jesus Way.
Hallelujah !

BE MAGNETS

If you love Jesus
Be a magnet !
Reflect God's glory.
Show your happiness,
Show enthusiasm,
Show love.
Be practical,
Full of action,
Smile as much as you can,
Even smiles do good !
Spread your joy
Be infectious !
Show your love of Jesus,
Speak about Him.
No preaching,
Just joy,

Enthusiasm is catching.
Be a magnet,
Draw people to you,
Then in time to Jesus.
You have power,
Power from the Holy Spirit.
You'll lose surface friends
But you'll make real friends.
Be on the look out,
Help and befriend.
Be adventurous,
Stay that way.
Never two days the same !
Keep your magnet strong,
It's sacred !
Hallelujah !

BEST FRIEND

Who is your best friend ?
Tom, Dick or Harry ?
Or Mary, Madge or Miriam ?
None of them !
For those with any sense,
No guessing,
It is Jesus Christ.
Even if right now
You deny this.
Jesus, Son of God,
He is alive today.
He died for you and me
To show His love.
Love for you.
Have sense,
Understand,
Accept Him.
He is your greatest friend.

Life long,
Everlasting.
You have worries ?
He'll help you !
Feel lost ?
He'll show the way.
Grieve over a passing ?
He'll comfort you.
Need a decision ?
He'll help direct.
All and so much more,
All through prayer.
Talk to your friend,
Do so now,
He waits for you,
His arms wide open.
Hallelujah

BETTER THAN A MILLION

Want to be a millionaire ?
Sounds good !
Think what you could do !
Comfort, ease, luxury.
Now slow down,
Get real !
No more dreaming.
Pick up the Bible.
Jesus met the rich.
They could not agree,
Agree to give their wealth away.
They could not understand
Spiritual wealth.
The wealth everlasting
That goes to eternal life.
It's the joy,
The joy of following Jesus.

It's the expectations
Of the promised Kingdom..
Worldly wealth,
It never lasts.
Our worldly life
It is temporary.
Life with Jesus,
It is permanent,
It is eternal.
Follow Him,
Stay with Him.
Escape the humdrum,
Live your new life,
It is guaranteed !
Be spiritually wealthy.
Hallelujah !

BETTER THAN SERMONS

Sermons are spiritual food.
We digest the best bits
They are good for us.
Thousand of sermons,
Some full of meat,
Others may be a bit weak
Yet we can thrive.
Thrive on that food.
We sit,
We listen,
Then what do we do ?
Sadly many do nothing !
But it can nourish,
Bring dedication,
Even spur us to action.
Pin point texts,
Mark them for use.
Use your Bible,
Mark in good texts.

Sermons alone
They will be forgotten.
Texts are remembered.
If a sermon directs you
Make notes.
The Bible points the way,
Often directs you
More than sermons do.
Aim to spend time,
Time and energy
Using your Bible.
Move texts into action,
Actions for Christ.
They are better than sermons !
But remember,
Spiritual food is in sermons,
Be on your toes,
Be alive !
Hallelujah !

BLESSED OR DEPRESSED ?

Which is best ?
Obviously being blessed !
Yet so many are depressed,
Few are blessed !
It's tragic !
It's pitiful !
Most go their own ways,
The life they want.
Amusements, clubs
Entertainments,
All to fight boredom.
Purposeless,
Pointless.
It's fine until trouble comes.
Illness, bereavement,
Debts, unemployment,

Marriage problems
And a lot more.
So much need not happen.
Run a prayer line
A hot line !
Christians have faith,
Have fun,
Have joy-full lives.
Blessed and not depressed.
Filled with friendship,
Filled with action,
Filled with purpose.
They have real life,
Be part of it,
Right now.
Hallelujah !

BLOOD DONORS

Millions give blood,
Give it freely,
No charge.
To save lives,
It's great.
They are helping so many.
Keep doing it !
Then turn your eyes to Jesus,
He came to save our lives.
He knew He would die,
He gave us His life,
No charge.
It was giving His love.
Love for all of us.
Sacrificial.

His blood a gift to us,
To everyone,
Millions have responded.
Saved from Hell.
To those whom He saves,
We should pay our debt,
Become life savers.
No sitting,
No dawdling,
Our task is urgent.
We can never repay everything,
Therefore be on your feet,
Be serving your Lord.
No hesitating.
Hallelujah !

BUSY BEES

Have you ever watched bees ?
They work non-stop.
Into a flower,
Out with pollen,
To another and another,
Always on the go.
Christians !
Learn from those bees !
Keep on the move,
Keep meeting people,
Keep showing love.
Love in action.
Love that witnesses,
Love that cares.
Show Jesus,

Never tire of loving others.
Now bees do rest,
They go to their hives.
Christians gain strength
Going to church
Going to worship.
Refreshed with prayer,
With fellowship,
Their batteries are recharged.
Then out again
Helped by the Holy Spirit.
You have the stamina,
It's God-given.
Thank Him.
Hallelujah !

CALL A SPADE A SPADE

You need to be honest.
Speaking as a Christian.
Jesus was blunt,
He said once,
"I will spit out the lukewarm".
You have to face facts.
The Bible tells His Word.
Unbelievers risk going to hell.
They are rejected.
Always be truthful.
Be positive.
Dwell on the good news,
The Gospels.
Dwell on God's promises.
Never be negative,
Stay with the positive.
Such good news !
A life of love,

A life of friendship,
A life everlasting,
Eternal life.
Jesus preached love,
No threats.
Go for God's words
The truth,
Where that fails
Go to prayer.
Keep on serving,
Go the second mile,
Spend and be spent
For Jesus sake.
Your good news
It can beat hell.
Stay a life saver.
Hallelujah !

CLEVER DEVIL

Believe in the devil !
He is real.
He's wanting you.
He never gives up.
Jesus met him,
Judas fell for him,
Yet many don't believe,
Don't believe he exists.
Wherever you live,
Sin is there.
It's everywhere.
Teenage bravado,
Vandalism,
Greed and dishonesty,
The list is long

And the devil claps his hands.
Nations in strife
Within and without.
Give the devil his due,
He is a clever devil.
Remember what Jesus said,
"Get thee behind me satan".
Repeat that daily !
No one is free from danger.
Praise God !
The devil runs !
God will hold you safe.
Stay close,
You will beat the devil.
Hallelujah !

COLD MASHED POTATOES

Horrible food !
Cold mashed potatoes.
Unwanted food.
Some Christians are similar !
They go to church,
Their special pew.
Pew sitters.
People that do nothing.
Appeals go unheeded,
Planned actions ignored,
Leaving all to others.
They stagnate.
Their church,
God's messages,
Sermonic urgings,
All leave them cold.

Nothing inspires,
Passive Christians.
Such a terrible waste !"
Pray for them,
Befriend them,
They are spiritually lonely,
Give them warmth.
God helping,
Change them !
They need your help,
They need to know Jesus.
They can change,
Be transformed,
Go for victory !
Hallelujah !

CROSS OVER

In your heart
You may know your life is bad.
You may have drifted,
Life has soured..
You've lost joy,
Enthusiasm has gone.
You know you have to change.
Change a lot.
Give up bad habits,
Sweep away flotsam,
Get rid of laziness.
You tell a Christian friend,
Tell him changing is hard.
You find this a good move.
Both sit down and pray.
It's a start,
It's a fresh effort..
You realise you have much to gain.

You just have to cross over.
Cross over to good sense.
Leave the senseless way,
Leave the useless ways.
Go for the Godly ways.
Know for sure the gains,
Happiness,
Permanent friends,
Meaningful habits
From the road to hell
To the road to Heaven,
To glorious eternity.
Ponder no more,
Cross over,
Now, not later.
Kneel down to Jesus !
Hallelujah !

DEAD CERTAIN !

It can mean a lot
Or mean nothing at all
It's a statement
It goes two ways.
For the unbeliever,
Bluntly,
They are on the road to hell.
For the believer
It is so much more,
They are on the road to Heaven.
Either way both are certain.
But the believing way,
What a difference !
Living with Jesus !
Certain to have eternal life.
Dead certain.
Then about fence sitters,
Sadly you risk hell.
Fall off your fence,
Fall the wrong side,
You are finished.

Nominal non-active Christians,
Do not take Heaven for granted !
Most people live temporary lives,
Artificial enjoyment,
Purposeless lives,
Selfish lives
Inward looking.
Ignoring their Creator.
Those who love the Lord,
We are commanded,
"Go out"
"Be fishers"
"Save, rescue, convert !"
We are duty bound,
Bringing folk to Jesus.
We will serve our Lord,
Serve Him without question,
Serve Him always.
Thank you Lord,
This is a privilege.
Hallelujah !

DEAD OR ALIVE

How do you reckon ?
Are you dead or alive ?
Sounds strange !
But just wait.
Life is very important.
Our real life on earth.
Real life is with Jesus.
An absolute fact.
Become a dedicated person,
You become brand new !
Then there are "the dead".
Spiritually dead.
Sadly most people.
Living temporary lives.
God made them,
They have great potential,
Hidden talents,
God-given possibilities,
All corroding away.

They are like cars
Rusting away on a dump.
Their future ?
Without Jesus ?
They are worthless.
That is why Jesus came to earth.
He came to wake us up.
To bring truth and love.
To show us God's Way.
To give us a second chance.
He taught us to tell others.
May we burn with eagerness,
May we serve to the full,
Jesus died for us,
We must not count the cost,
Just go flat out.
Thank you Jesus !
Hallelujah !

DO NOT DILUTE

Sometimes it's a fact
Preachers preach too gently.
They use God's words
Use them with gloves on !
Many never mention hell !
They tell of God's love,
The Christmas story,
The Easter story,
Of parables and Pentecost.
Familiar messages,
Lovingly, meaningful.
Too often forgotten by Monday.
God's words must stand out !
Firmly show the positives,
Firmly show the negatives,
Nothing hidden.

The joy of following,
The darkness of failure.
Preaching with bold love
Yet warning of pitfalls.
Making that extra effort,
Stirring their listeners.
Then often -
Challenging congregations,
Setting Godly aims.
God's Word,
It must not be diluted.
It must not be tailored,
It must stand out.
Plainly,
Blessedly.
Hallelujah !

DON'T LOOK BACK !

You found Christ,
Such a great event !
It's made the difference,
You have a new life.
Even so you sometimes ponder,
Think of old times.
Entertainments,
Night life,
Dubious events.
How come such thoughts ?
It's all from the devil !
Trying to lead you astray.
He lost you once,
He wants you back !

Beat him !
Right away -
Talk to Jesus.
You'll win every time.
Keep on the course,
Know Jesus as your friend,
He never leaves you,
If you think He is far away
It is you who moved away.
Back on course,
Back to joy,
Back to happiness,
Back to spiritual love
Hallelujah !

DOWN AND OUT

You're living your life,
Living it your way.
Having high times.
Possibly being immoral.
You have excitement,
There is glamour,
Then suddenly you crash !
Everything goes wrong.
You are in a mess.
At your wits end.
You feel down and out.
You cannot get up,
You cannot get sorted.
Now listen,
Listen hard !
There is a way out,
Not an easy way
But a sure way.

Get a Bible,
Read the Gospels,
Take time,
Concentrate.
Then pray !
You cannot pray ?
You certainly can !
Picture Jesus,
With eyes shut or open
You talk to Him.
Tell Him your troubles.
Believe that Jesus listens,
He definitely does.
Ask for forgiveness,
Be sincere.
Jesus waits right now.
Start your new life,
Hallelujah !

DYING TO LOVE YOU

Give it lots of thought,
Jesus died for you.
Realise it,
Picture it.
It is very true.
Ask yourself,
Have you paid your debt ?
He gave Himself,
Are you giving yourself ?
Giving through service ?
Jesus taught us so much.
That God cares,
Cares for everyone.
We are told so many times,
Told in His Word.

Jesus bring God so near.
It cost Him His life,
Hung on a cross.
Sacrificial love.
We cannot sit back !
He saved you and me,
Saved so we could save others.
We can never repay to the full
But we can do so much.
Enjoy the adventure,
Enjoy the challenge,
Enjoy the obstacles
For Jesus is with you.
Hallelujah !

FAITH-FULL

You cannot be a Christian,
Cannot follow Jesus
Unless you have faith.
Total belief,
Totally certain.
If you believe you have faith.
Faith that Jesus lives.
Faith that He loves you.
Faith that He cares.
The greater your belief
The greater your faith.
Reading The Bible,
Praying every day,
Fellowshipping with others,
It all adds to more faith.

Believe in Him,
When in trouble,
When with grief,
When depressed.
Trust at all times,
Let nothing block your way.
Know Him,
Love Him,
Worship Him.
There are no limits.
Be faith-full,
It is so wonderful !
Thank the Lord for faith.
Hallelujah !

FOR THE HURTING

Have you ever been hurt ?
Badly let down ?
Deserted by friends ?
You feel devastated.
You are depressed,
You feel alone.
It's a dark tunnel.
All alone ?
No way so !
You are never alone !
Jesus never left you -
You forgot Him !
Pour out your misery,
Share your problems.
Gradually,

Slowly
Darkness turns to light.
Picture Jesus,
Imagine youself hand in hand,
Actually holding your Saviour !
You'll feel His love,
You'll know He cares.
Picture Him smiling !
Your hurts are healing
And you even smile !
Give Jesus your thanks,
Cling to Him,
Never let go again,
He is everything.
Hallelujah !

FROM THE BEGINNING

My life,
It started on nothing,
It was on "empty"
Until God took over.
Gradually,
Imperceptibly,
Bit by bit
Without me knowing
Things began to change.
I thought I made all decisions,
I thought I was in charge.
I think God was smiling !
Friends had prayed for me
And God was responding.
His plans for me,
The ones pre-ordained,

They began to emerge.
I woke up,
Woke up spiritually.
I accepted Christ,
I asked Him to take over.
And now ?
It is a daily adventure.
New aims,
New targets,
Action and service.
Surely God smiles now !
Listen to me,
Never take charge,
God leads,
We follow.
Hallelujah !

FULL TIMERS

Be a full timer.
Full time for Jesus.
Unpaid
But with a golden future..
A heavenly future.
It's strange
Working for Jesus.
No clock watching
Yet time flies.
So do the days.
It's nothing like other jobs.
There is variety galore.
At times adventures,
At times sadness,
At other times joy.
Then our workmates.

The best anywhere.
All dedicated,
All loving,
All helping each other.
Coming to Jesus
It's a full time promise.
No idling,
Always on the look out,
Always ready to witness,
Always totally alert,
Saving lives.
What a great time !
Just one MUST -
You MUST be a full timer.
Hallelujah !

GET OFF YOUR THRONE

Let us face it,
Admit the truth !
We all have had our own kingdoms.
We have ruled,
We have been in charge.
What we do,
What we think,
What we say
All from ourselves.
Basically selfish,
Basically self-centred.
Get real !
Who made you ?
Who is really King ?
GOD !
So you've goofed !

Wake up to reality,
Get off your throne,
It never was yours !
It belongs to God,
You belong to God,
Be real !
Ask God to take over,
Right now.
To run your life.
Speak with Him,
Work with Him.
Move into your new life,
Your life with God.
Keep on His Way,
The Eternal Way.
Hallelujah !

GET LOST SATAN

Jesus our Saviour,
He was tempted by Satan.
His reply we know,
"Get thee behind me",
In other words
"Get lost Satan".
The devil is very real,
With us every day
And so many don't believe it.
Every bad thought,
Envy, Greed,
Impurity,
Impatience
And so much more,

All from Satan.
He will not give up.
It happened to Jesus,
It happens to all.
Do as Jesus did,
Tell him to get lost.
Then keep with Jesus.
When Satan nudges
Always turn to Jesus.
Satan hates it,
Jesus loves it.
Keep on doing it,
Always.
Hallelujah !

GET ON BOARD

Imagine,
You're at a station,
You linger with a friend.
The guard yells
"Get on board!",
You nearly missed the train.
Life can be like that.
So many linger,
Loving themselves.
They are fence sitters.
They know about Jesus,
Know He is right
Yet they linger.
Reluctant to move,
Unready to board
They procrastinate.
There is no guard,
There are no shouts

And many turn away.
God calls everyone,
The call is heard,
It's the the thought,
Right or wrong.
Take the right call,
You're on the move,
Take the wrong call
You're falling down.
God calls,
Hear Him in the Bible,
Hear Him from friends,
Hear Him in church.
Do not linger,
Get on board,
Board the Godly train,
Travel the holy track.
Hallelujah !

GET UP AGAIN !

There is a saying,
"Fall down seven times
Get up eight times".
Christians are not perfect,
We've all fallen,
One time or another.
Admit it !
Some may be little trips,
Others heavy falls.
It's hard to avoid all sin.
You have to battle,
Keep on your feet.
There is help,
There is comfort.
God helps,
God forgives.

Forgives the truly repentant.
And God knows your mind.
God is our Father,
We are His children,
Follow and obey.
The road may be rocky,
Keep on with prayer.
Prayer will keep you walking,
Thank God for His help.
Stay close, very close,
Satan will be kept at bay.
If you fall
Then cry to Jesus.
Trust in Him always.
Hallelujah !

GLITTER OR GLOW

Do you aim to enjoy life ?
The secular life,
The artificial life ?
Wanting to be noticed,
Attending social highs,
Cocktail parties a norm.
The glittering façade.
Aimless pursuits
Through the hardening glitter.
The social round,
Knowing the right people !
Totally artificial.
Change over,
Go the best way !
The Christian way.

Experience Christian fellowship,
It's warm,
It's genuine.
It's full of value.
It's supportive,
Helpful,
Happy and secure.
Learn to serve Jesus,
Be adventurous,
Go the second mile,
Jesus as your companion,
Jesus as your friend.
You've grown up !
You're a new person !
Hallelujah !

GLOOM-OMETER

Some Christians are bad,
Bad examples !
Long gloomy faces,
Cheerless.
Puts people off !
It's the opposite of witness !
Makes folk disbelieve.
Such Christians need help !
Urgent help.
They are spoiling the scene,
Really bad examples.
They've lost out.
Forgotten the good news,
The Gospel news.
Of Jesus' love.
So they live in the gloom.
Doing nothing,

Stagnating.
Stir them up !
Infiltrate enthusiasm !
Set them alight.
Tell them Jesus wants them,
Wants them to spread joy.
Pray with them,
Ask for His help.
No more gloom,
Into pure Christian joy.
Become Spirit-filled,
Striving as one,
Saving the lost,
Showing happiness,
Shining all the way.
Hallelujah !

GODLY BLUES

Being a Christian,
Loving Jesus as Lord,
It brings happiness,
It leads to eternal life.
Yet there are other times,
Times of sadness,
Call it "Godly Blues"!
Godly blues do not last.
Talk with God,
Talk with other Christians,
The blues will fade away
For the countless people,
Those ignoring God,
Those who reject God
Spurning His Message
It's a sadness.

Almost insoluble.
Permanent blues.
Troubles and gloom
With no way through.
They can be saved !
Jesus told us we must.
Work with Jesus,
One by one.
All of us.
We must obey,
We must be dedicated.
Break the pagan blues
Singing to the Lord.
Let the saints go marching in !
Hallelujah !

GOOD ENOUGH

Some of us Christians,
We are full of excuses.
"We are not good enough"
"We cannot talk"
"We don't know how to start"
And they are defeatists.
Feeble reasons,
Ways to hide away.
Paul said in Ephesians,
"I am the most useless Christian".
Then he thanked the Lord,
Thanked Him for using him.
Be like Paul,
Humble but active.
Ever get tempted ?
That is not a sin,
Even Jesus was tempted.
The sin is falling down.
Those who are with excuses,
Those excuses verge on sin.

Jesus commands us,
"Be fishers of men"
Sharing God's love.
No room for excuses,
No chance to hide,
You cannot hide from God.
Face the facts,
All of us,
We are imperfect,
But we can all be used.
Arm yourself with prayer,
Know you have a privilege
Serving Jesus.
Know you are called,
Called by name.
You are in His Team.
You are good enough,
Jesus calls you.
Rejoice !
Hallelujah !

GOD'S KEY

God's key is faith.
Take it.
Use it always.
Faith is needed,
Without it you are lost.
Read Hebrews Chapter 11,
"Now faith is being sure,
Sure of what we hope for,
Certain of what we do not see".
Without faith you have nothing,
There is no hope,
There is no joy,
There is no love,
There is no eternal life.
We are lost !
With faith
Everything changes.

Heavenly doors open.
Our lives are great,
Our future is certain.
Faith is wonderful,
Faith is life changing,
Faith is life.
It is endless,
It is miraculous,
And it is for all.
Take it fully now,
It's God's key for you,
It's your key,
The doors are open,
Use it,
Travel the heavenly way.
Hallelujah !

GOD'S REDWOODS

Redwoods and Sequoias,
God's greatest trees.
Redwoods stand for 2000 years,
Sequoias up to 3000 years.
God's giants.
God created the world,
He made those trees.
Living proof of God's work.
No man can ever copy these.
They stand in glory,
Living towers to 300 feet.
Strong,
Resilient,
Almost out of this world.
Yet even greater
He made you and me.

We must strive like redwoods
To be strong,
To be resilient
And be wonderful examples,
Examples of our Father God.
We can go a step further,
We can have eternal life.
Life beyond our dreams.
We all have a purpose,
We must respond,
Be filled with the Holy Spirit,
Stronger than even God's trees.
Go for it,
Go flat out,
God is so great !
Hallelujah !

GOLIATHS

Everyone regardless
We have Goliaths to kill.
No one can claim
Life is obstacle free.
Just like the boy David
All must be brave.
When we accept Jesus
We know Him as our Saviour,
We have killed a pagan Goliath
With the act of coming to Jesus.
We battle against temptation
Goliath beaten again.
Our old ways,
They cling like barnacles,
Hard to shift,

We slay another Goliath.
We go to prayer
And we win with Jesus.
There will be more Goliaths
But now we will win.
Goliaths of greed,
Of selfishness,
Of more temptations,
All defeated.
Thank you Lord Jesus,
You are the victor,
Your are our Saviour,
We hold your hand.
Hallelujah !

GONE TO THE DOGS

From the Bible
Read about the prodigal son.
We say
"He went to the dogs".
He was finished,
He had shot his bolt.
On the way to hell.
He had spent all his funds,
He had been with prostitutes,
He ended up feeding pigs,
And eating their swill.
It happens to many,
Going broke,
Living useless lives.
Some call them wastrels.
Don't jump to conclusions !
God loves everyone.
Jesus said,
"Judge not lest you be judged".

Jesus loves wastrels.
They can be saved.
They need help,
The help of Christians.
They must be befriended,
Told of a new life,
Helped and advised,
Shown how to repent,
To come to Jesus,
Changing through prayer.
They must know they are loved,
Must know there is a future,
A good future.
Seek them out,
Bring them to Christ,
Gone to the dogs ?
No, have them go to Jesus.
Hallelujah !

GREAT EXPECTATIONS

It is wonderful,
It is so great,
Being active,
Active for Jesus !
It is a daily adventure,
Being ready to serve.
Nothing can beat it,
Looking for souls,
Helping happily,
Belonging to Jesus.
Knowing He lives,
Knowing He is so close.
Being positive,
Worshipping,
Praying,
Rejoicing in the future.

Those who serve for Jesus,
All have great expectations,
All look forward,
Being led by their Saviour.
Great expectations
Of going to His Kingdom,
Of seeing the Lord,
Seeing Him face to face.
What a privilege !
Active for Jesus,
Above anything else,
Share the joy,
Share the privilege,
Share Jesus !
Expect great things !
Hallelujah !

HAND PICKED

When Jesus began His ministry
It was by Galilee.
He hand picked disciples.
The fishermen,
A tax collector,
The rest one by one.
Rough countrymen,
A few more educated.
A team of twelve.
Hand picked.
"Follow me" He said.
They gave up all,
They followed Him.
Right now,
Today,
The call still comes,
"Follow Me" Jesus says.
It's a message for us who believe,
For us to mature,
To give up any wasteful ways.

It's a message to the world,
We must spread this message.
Jesus started with twelve.
That call has continued,
Millions have heard it,
All are hand picked.
Jesus know all,
Name by name.
It is a miracle,
Miracles happen every day,
Be part of those miracles.
Go out,
See your friends,
Witness,
Rejoice to them
Tell them Jesus is the greatest,
Tell them they need Him,
Bring them in !
Hallelujah !

HAVE A FAITH-LIFT

To many of us -
We know of Jesus,
We say we accept Him.
How would we score
If on a "Faithometer"?
Knowing about Jesus,
It is not enough.
We must be faith-full.
Heaps of it !
Real belief equals real faith,
Unshaken faith.
Don't be a doubting Thomas !
Faith is caught not taught.
Caught from others.
Jesus scolded His disciples
When faith was lacking.
Faith starts small,

It grows,
It matures,
It becomes solid.
It will fill your life.
Completely.
Knowing about Jesus,
Go much further !
Love Jesus
Then you will have faith.
It combats Satan,
It will help direct you.
Need more ?
Then go to prayer,
You will find it !
Pray and pray and pray,
You'll feel the answer.
Hallelujah !

HAVE A "GOD DAY"

You want a God-Day ?
Then you can have one !
Not just one day
But every day.
Be aware,
Your every thought,
Your every word,
Your every action
God knows ahead of you !
Start the day,
"Good Morning Jesus"
Then really pray.
Know His presence,
Talk as friend to friend.
Continue during the day.
See around you people,
They are His people.

Look for troubled faces,
Say an extra prayer.
Passing a church ?
Send a brief prayer,
A prayer for it's members.
Any church.
Thank God for it's witness.
See an ambulance ?
Pray for the crew,
Pray for the sick or injured.
Such days you live with Jesus,
Such days are "God Days.
Then at the end of the day
Tired and ready for sleep,
"Good Night Lord"
And a prayer of thanks.
Hallelujah !

HELL

Ever heard your preacher
Preach about hell ?
You may have done
But most have not !
It is a subject avoided.
It's too bad !
Almost unmentionable..
Yet The Bible tells us much.
We are warned of hell,
We are told to battle evil.
We are to be alert.
The dangers can be blatant.
Hell is really real
On earth and on death.
Yet it is often glossed over.
It's just too scary.
Read God's Word,
Understand

And be fearless.
Fight temptations.
Get close to God,
Keep on His Way.
Choose God not hell !
Seems obvious,
But do not go astray.
God is powerful,
He protects us,
When we are on His team.
The Lord changes dark into light.
Love for us all,
Satan and hell are beaten,
Stay firm,
You've beaten hell.
Praise the Lord
Hallelujah !

HE KNOWS

We are talking of Jesus,
That's who knows.
Have no doubt,
He knows everything.
What has happened,
What is happening
And what will happen.
He knows your future,
He knows the day He returns,
Everything.
Psalm 139 will explain..
You will understand.
Clear out the dross,

Inspect yourselves !
Cleanse yourselves.
The Lord is positive,
He know your good ways,
He knows your good work,
He know your love,
He loves testimonies.
He loves the seeds you plant,
All will be remembered.
Just keep on striving,
Doing your best,
He will know !
Hallelujah!

HEY EVERYBODY !

You've got to listen,
Give me five minutes !
I'm not selling goods,
I've no politics,
I'm just bowled over !
Struck all of a heap !
Because of Jesus !
I laughed at Christians,
I scorned their churches,
Then it happened.
My best friend found Christ.
I was shocked,
I was dismayed.
He told me he was changed,
He was born again !
My best friend a Christian !
He made me sit up.
He told me to listen hard.
Talked of a man called Paul.
He hated Christians,
He persecuted them,
Until God spoke to him
On the road to Damascus.
Changed him into a Christian.
My friend went on,

He was so different,
Truly changed,
Really sincere.
Paul became Christ's superman,
My friend was won over.
He told me how Jesus died,
How Paul gave his life.
I felt I was foolish,
I wanted to know more.
I joined my friend in prayer,
It was a beginning,
The next day I learnt more,
I was convinced.
Being convinced,
That is not enough,
I have to share my joy,
Listen, the Lord calls you,
Every one of you.
Don't just listen,
Be convinced,
Believe,
Be active for Jesus,
Keep on sharing,
Sharing your Saviour.
Hallelujah !

HORROR-SCOPES

Read the newspapers,
Almost any magazine,
There will be a feature,
Called Horoscopes.
Written by fools
Fooling millions.
So many who are gullible.
They believe daily forecasts,
They believe weekly ones,
Monthly ones.
Totally pagan.
Totally false,
It is work of the devil..
Millions blinded with lies.
Luck is a pagan word,
Good or bad it is wrong.
Be sensible !
There is only one Way,
God's Way.
Read His Word,

Ignore "Horror-scopes".
What you read in The Bible,
That is what is true,
Look nowhere else !
Believe in Jesus,
Utterly,
Believe in The Holy Spirit,
Know what is promised.
Be aware,
Look forward,
The wonderful,
The glorious,
The terrific
Eternal life.
God's awesome Kingdom.
Never never read Horror-scopes -
Run to God,
He's with you.
Hallelujah !

HOW MANY SCALPS ?

For every Christian,
Putting it crudely,
How many scalps have you ?
Meaning one thing,
How many changed lives,
How many with your actions.
How many now love Jesus ?
From seeds you planted.
One thing is true,
We never know on some seeds,
They can take a long time,
A long time to grow.
Counting is not important,
The key to everything
It's dedication.
That is what counts.
We never know results.
Leave that to God.

Christians must be active,
We must live God's way,
We must love,
We must help the helpless.
Actions are better than words,
Actions speak volumes.
How much have you done ?
Keep planting your seeds,
Seeds of love,
God is the gardener,
He is in charge.
Just be happy,
Happy to serve Jesus,
Happy to love Him,
Happy to share Him.
Just go on loving Jesus !
Hallelujah !

HUMPTY DUMPTY

Humpty Dumpty sat on a wall,
Humpty Dumpty had a great fall.
There are millions of them !
So many that fall.
Life seemed so great,
So much to enjoy.
But not good lives.
Tawdry lives,
Lives filled with trivia,
Lives tinged with badness.
Money wasted,
No thought for others,
Filled with nothing-ness !
The highs have been great,
Then come the lows.
Wrong decisions,
Wrong kind of friends,
Financial worries,
Marital worries.
The world seems to crumble.
Nothing seems right.
Look back,
Not much to see,

Nothing important.
Gather your senses.
You can change,
There is a silver lining,
It's not too late !
Your God -
God who you have ignored,
He still loves you.
Give this some thought,
Realise you have done wrong.
Seek help.
A Christian friend,
A church,
Definitely your Bible.
Jump off the wall,
Jump to Jesus !
Come to your senses,
Look forward,
Forward to a new life.
A life you will enjoy,
A new world,
A heavenly world.
Hallelujah !

I DID IT MY WAY

So goes a well known song.
Sung by a well known star.
It's true !
Most of the world does this !
They all go their way !
What a tragedy !
It reflects sinful ways.
Self-centredness,
Selfishness,
Greed.
It's me and me and me again.
Yet God made us,
And not to live that way.
Jesus told us,
"Love your neighbour",
"Go the second mile",
"Tend the sick",

"Tell others"
And so much more !
Jesus showed examples,
Washing of feet,
Sympathy for the sick,
Love for the outcast.
He worked hard,
Nothing for Himself,
Everything for others.
Then the supreme sacrifice,
Dying on a cross,
Showing His love.
Sing a new song,
A better song,
"We'll do it God's Way"
Again and again and again.
Hallelujah !

IMAGINATION

Reading God's Word,
The stories of Moses,
Of Samson,
Of David and Samuel
And so many more
Then stop,
Think !
Imagine.
Picture the exploits,
Picture Daniel with the lions,
Zacheus up a tree,
The feeding of the five thousand.
God stands out,
Time and time again.
Picture Jesus in the manger,
The flight to Egypt,
Jesus as a boy.
His disciples,
Stormy Galilee.
Dusty roads and crowds,

The hustle and bustle,
The cries and shouts.
Then Jesus' trial.
The crucifixion,
The empty tomb
Imagine these scenes,
Make them vivid !
Feel you can hear Jesus,
His voice reaching all.
Then live it all !
Live what Jesus preached,
Live what God's Word tells.
All those pictures,
Those thoughts
Then realise Jesus lives today !
He is with you now,
His story for you never ends.
Share all this with friends,
Rejoice !
Hallelujah !

I'M HERE !

So patient,
So wonderful,
So loving
Is God our Father.
Whoever has trouble,
Whoever is depressed,
Whoever is lost
Meet God in prayer.
Gods says,"I'm here"!
He's just a prayer away.
At your wits end ?
God is there !
In a pit of despair ?
He is there !
He is everywhere.
Loving to help,

He is the greatest,
Just a prayer away.
He knows your troubles,
He's ahead of you !
Stop delaying,
Stop that gloom,
Go to God right now.
Shrink your worries,
It will happen !
Replaced by happiness,
Coming through to joy.
For God your Father says,
"I am here".
Respond right now
Shout Hallelujah !

IMPERFECT

Every one of us,
We are imperfect.
Whatever we do
We are still imperfect.
It's a challenge !
Also a warning.
Do not be discouraged.
Jesus said,
"Only my Father is perfect".
So every day just strive.
Strive to do better,
Strive to serve,
Strive to be loving,
Strive to care and help.
The more we do
The closer to Jesus.

The greater the peace.
Just accept the fact
You are not perfect !
Be positive !
You're in the Jesus Team.
Loving Jesus,
Loving those you meet,
Loving the second mile.
Belonging to Jesus.
Dedicated,
Enthusiastic.
And in return ?
You know God's love,
God loves the imperfect !
You and your friends.
Hallelujah !

IT'S HELL !

Don't be stupid !
It's hell without Jesus !
Realise this.
However successful you are,
However rich,
However things go,
It is all temporary.
It cannot last.
In the end it can be hell.
If you're without Jesus.
Our time on earth,
Just a life span,
But be aware
Life is eternal.
One way or another.
Which way do we go ?

It's obvious,
Go the Jesus Way.
Accept Him as Saviour.
Be born again.
The definite way,
The way to God's Kingdom,
To a holy eternal life.
Don't even think the pagan way.
There is no return.
Jesus waits for you,
He forgives,
He calls,
Answer Him,
Just do it !
Hallelujah !

JACKPOT !

You're with your friends.
Slot machine gambling.
Hooked on jackpots !
You watch,
Suddenly it happens,
A shower of cash,
The jackpot pays off !
A whole pile !
It's like a magnet.
You all want to try again.
So many machines,
So many jackpots !
Then most leave,
Leave with empty pockets.
Jackpots are rare.
Outside they meet a friend,
He is happy,
He tells them,
"I've hit the jackpot!",
He tells of Jesus,

Some walk away,
Others stay to listen.
He tells of despair,
Of unhappiness,
How Jesus filled the gap.
How life had changed,
From the dark to the light.
We listen to him,
We hear the clink of cash behind,
What to do ?
God gave us good sense.
Deep down that sense stirs.
Bring it out !
Listen, Take heed,
It's a life saver !
Follow that friend,
Then follow His Saviour,
You'll never forget,
You have been saved !
Hallelujah !

JESUS RECYCLES

Nobody on earth
Is past redemption.
Jesus died for all,
Not just you and me.
It's terrific !
Everyone needs Jesus,
We all need recycling !
To be born again.
Look at it this way,
God invented recycling !
He turns pagans
Into new persons.
Each of us,
We are recycled miracles.
He literally saves us,
Rescues us from hell.

From the Devil.
Believe in miracles,
Believe in that miracle.
Believe He loves you,
That you are His.
Then rejoice with action.
Sow seeds for Jesus.
Sow everywhere
Among your family,
Among your friends,
Just about anywhere.!
There are billions to save,
Just keep on planting !
Be filled with joy,
Hallelujah !

JOY-FULL

Coming to Christ
It changed my life.
It is fantastic !
Out of this world,
Into God's World.
It's joy-full !
Each day a new day,
I am never alone.
I know God loves everyone,
For He even loves me !
Now I must share Jesus,
His love overflows,
It is for all who will listen.
It is a challenge,
A challenge to rescue others.
He has filled my cup,
It overflows.

I pray for direction,
I pray to be used,
I pray for His help.
Opportunities will come,
Filling others with joy.
No Christian can be idle,
No believer can just sit.
Be filled with that joy,
Be filled with enthusiasm,
Be bursting to tell,
Tell of your Saviour.
Never stand still.
And age makes no difference,
All be on the Jesus Team.
Thank the Lord.
Hallelujah !

JUST DO IT !

Life can be boring,
Full of dead ends.
So many possibilities
And so little done.
Even some who follow Jesus
They do so little.
Get stirred up,
Change gear,
Be energised.
Get spiritual stamina.
Don't just think,
Just do it !
Do some helping,
Do some visiting,
Befriend the lonely,
Comfort the bereaved,
Maybe baby sit,
Maybe dig a garden.

Life boring ?
No way !
Be part of a church team,
Call it "The Jesus Team",
Then go His Way.
Ready for emergencies,
Ready to pray,
Ready to move out,
and your motto ?
JUST DO IT
You will make a difference.
Not just to you,
But to others,
To your church.
What you do
It will bear fruit.
Just do it !
Hallelujah !

KEEP FIT !

Everyone knows this,
You should keep fit !
Eat sensibly,
Exercise,
Take advice.
Physically all to the good.
Even more essential,
Spiritual fitness.
With daily exercise.
Start by praying,
Not a wish list,
Real prayers.
Hourly talk with Jesus.
That is not all.
Forget yourself.
Look on others,
Their needs,

Their well being.
Just as Jesus did,
Just as He does now.
Talk to people,
Let God lead.
You may make new friends.
You may save a soul.
Inspect yourself daily !
You have to be fit enough,
Fit enough for Jesus.
Fit to serve,
Fit to love,
Fit to witness.
This way life is great,
This way you're ready,
Spiritually fit !
Hallelujah !

KRAKATOA

In 1883 Krakatoa exploded,
An island in Indonesia,
A volcano.
The largest explosion recorded
That the world has ever known.
For over two years
There were ripple effects.
World wide.
Yet there is a bigger event !
One that has echoed,
Echoed for 2000 years.
It was Jesus born in a manger.
The Son of God,
The Saviour of the world.
He ministered for three years,
Three years and twelve disciples.
Teaching and preaching,
Loving and caring.
Unbelievably crucified,

Then rising from the dead.
The impossibles went on.
His message of God's love,
It never stopped,
It went on and on and on.
The ripple effect continues,
Billions love the Lord,
For He is alive,
He is among us !
It's not just a ripple,
Waves of love,
God omnipresent.
It is God's World.
Believe ion Him !
Rejoice !
Stay firm !
Let the waves wash over you.
Hallelujah !

LABEL-LESS

Most Christians have labels,
Baptist or Methodist,
Roman Catholic,
Pentecostal,
Episcopalian or Anglican.
There are many more.
Arguably, ways of worship.
Variations in belief.
But they all proclaim,
"God is love!".
"Jesus is Saviour!".
These days churches are closer,
Some unite at times.
There is more Christian fellowship.

Showing all are one in Christ.
But ways to worshipping
They are all treasured.
One thing is certain,
When we end our earthly stay,
When we reach the pearly gates
Our labels disappear !
No more divisions,
No more priests and pastors.
No Archbishops or bishops,
All are one in Christ.
Label-less
Citizens of His Kingdom.
Hallelujah !

LIFE INSURANCE

It's something to take out
For cash for your family.
No doubt helpful.
Real life insurance,
It is so different,
Far, far better !
It lasts eternally.
The cost ?
It's been paid for in full.
Paid by Jesus,
Paid for you.
Hanging from a cross,
Showing His love.
Almost to good to be true.
Almost incomprehensible.

The Son of God.
Dying for you and me.
Yet it is true !
Believe it !
Be filled with faith.,
You have a promise,
Eternal heavenly life.
Everlasting life insurance.
Act fast,
Cast off sin,
Disown bad secular ways,
Do not procrastinate,
Now is the time !
Hallelujah !

LIKE AN ICEBERG

You are like an iceberg !
You and your friends,
People around you
They only see an eighth of you !
The rest is hidden !
We all try and impress.
Maybe a smiling face,
Friendly words,
Helpful hands.
Good ways indeed.
We can look good,
But what are we like underneath ?
Pure or impure ?
Are we true Christians

Or are we surface Christians ?
Busy for Jesus
Or hypocrites ?
Positive or negative ?
Our hidden parts,
Jesus knows them.
Be sure they are good,
A Christian through and through.
Be willing to be open,
Nothing hidden.
For being a good Christian,
You are a little Christ !
Hallelujah !

LIVE IT, LOVE IT

It is fun,
Being a Christian !
It's an adventure,
It's challenging
Being a Christian.
Life cannot be dull.
Where is the fun ?
It is in the closeness of Jesus.
What adventure ?
It's new things each day.
How come challenging ?
Why man, you have to fight !
Fight scorn,
Fight opposition
All in a positive way.
Living like Christ,
Loving it,

You're in a sacred team !
A team that loves and cares.
An all age team.
All are active,
All seek out the lost,
Sharing Jesus,
Bringing joy from Jesus.
We act as one,
We do our best,
We like it,
We love it,
We thank the Lord,
We praise Him.
Come on in !
Join us now,
Like it and love it !
Hallelujah !

LUKE WARM

Stop being luke warm !
Even Jesus disliked this.
Half-hearted Christians,
People who do little.
They do not witness,
They do little to serve.
They travel their own way.
Luke warm.
Jesus said,
"I spit them out !".
He spoke very plainly.
Being a Christian
It is either fully so
Or you are a failure.
Pew sitters,
Fence sitters,
The frozen chosen,

They never know Jesus,
At least not to the full.
If you know Jesus
You cannot sit still !
You cannot do nothing !
Christians are dedicated,
They are equipped,
They are eager
Enthusiastic,
Set on fire by the Holy Spirit,
Red hot and active.
Join God's labourers.
This must be your way,
Do not miss out,
Belong to Jesus !
Hallelujah!

MAKE A DIFFERENCE

Some call it M_A_D !
"Make a difference".
In yourself,
In your friends,
With those you meet.
The Christian way.
You have a mission,
Bringing folk to Jesus,
Saving the lost
And following Jesus.
Start with your friends,
Then on to prayer,
Then to doing.
Strive hard,
Much depends on you.
Heaven or hell !
Aim for close contacts,
Aim to speak frankly,
To speak with purpose,
Just how Jesus expects,

How He makes a difference.
Lives that are changed.
Have them feel sincerity,
That you really care,
That you are serious,
Serious about Jesus.
Know they need to change,
Know they have a great future,
Know that they are important.
Be positive,
Be prayer-filled,
Spend time,
Be patient
Jesus is with you.
Keep with your mission,
Making things different.
Thank God for your help,
Thank God for results.
Hallelujah !

MIND BOGGLING !

The Bible says,
"Jesus loves us".
Billions of us !
Even so,
He loves us one by one,
Name by name !
It seems way out !
Those with sense
They have no doubt.
It's true !
Just as The Bible is true.
We can feel His presence,
We've been born again.
New minds,
New lives,
New ways.

It's mind boggling !
Open The Bible,
See what God says.
Add faith to understanding,
Trust God's Word.
God is great,
Creator of every living thing,
Creator of the universe.
He made all,
He knows all,
And he loves you !
It is a wonder,
It is mind boggling.
Praise Him,
Thank Him.
Hallelujah !

MIRACLES

You'd better believe !
Believe in miracles,
As miracles happen,
They happen every day.
Big ones and small ones,
It is God at work.
It started with Creation.
It went on to the Holy Land.
Sending His Son.
Healing miracles,
The Resurrection,
The Ascension.
Then with twelve disciples
His Church began.
It grew,
It multiplied.
From the twelve
To Billions.
Each believer a miracle.

Miracles worldwide.
Then what about us ?
Each of us a miracle.
Every good thing,
They all come from God.
We have victories,
Bringing some to Jesus.
More miracles.
God given gifts.
All of us -
We experience miracles.
God loves impossibilities,
Miracles happen !
Thank you God,
Whatever is done we thank you.
And Lord,
Thank you for eternity.
Hallelujah !

MIRRORS

We all use mirrors.
Not just the ladies.
What do we see ?
We see our outsides.
What goes on inside ?
How do we look ?
How does Jesus see us ?
He sees our spiritual side,
A different picture.
He knows you inside out.
Nothing hidden.
Being good looking,
That counts for nothing.
Being ugly – it does not count.
What counts is inside.
For us we find it hard,

Hard to see our spiritual self.
Think hard,
Try and check your positives,
Count your negatives
And turn to God in prayer.
Pray to sweep out the negatives,
To increase the positives.
Then later,
Check again,
Positives and negatives.
They are the spiritual mirror.
Keep trying,
Keep out the negatives.
Shine for Jesus,
Your mirror is good !
Hallelujah !

MISSING !

What is missing ?
Go to most churches -
People are missing,
Many have empty pews.
It has been so for years.
It is getting worse.
Shrinking churches.
So little done.
Incredible !
An insult to God !
Bewildering !
How come ?
Members lack enthusiasm,
Lack faith,
Lack purpose,
Lack leadership.
What else ?
Pure dedication.
Lack of praying,
Lack of prayer meetings.
Lack of cell meetings.

And this need not be !
It must not be !
Neglect is sinful.
Bring back God's Word !
Be led to fish,
Be led to serve,
Be led into action.
Move into urgent plans,
Red alert plans,
Godly plans..
Revival WILL HAPPEN !
Inject enthusiasm.
Pastors and members alike.
Let none escape !
It is possible,
It is God's will,
Believe with extra faith.
You'll see His miracles I
If you now accept His Way !
Hallelujah !

MONDAY CHRISTIANS

Never heard of Monday Christians ?
Learn about them now !
Think of a full church,
Christians on a Sunday.
How many worship on the Monday ?
How many fish for souls on Monday?
And on each day ?
How many really pray on Mondays ?
Thank God some really do.
Mondays, week days,
They are busy days.
Be sure,
Be certain,
Make room for Jesus !
Be Monday Christians.
It's a test for a Christian,
Through the hustle and bustle
Giving time to Jesus.

He must have top priority.
Executives or labourers,
Women workers or housewives,
All to be Monday Christians.
Take Jesus to work,
Have Jesus in your kitchen,
In your workshop.
Every day a Godly day.
No day can be less..
Let not an hour go by,
Go with Jesus.
Show your Christian love,
Do not leave it at home.
Follow this,
Expect a glowing week,
Shining for Jesus.
Hallelujah !

MOUNTAIN MOVER

Every active Christian,
No exceptions,
All have met the Mountain Mover.
All of have had troubles,
Who moved them ?
Jesus, the Mountain Mover.
Those without Christ
They have no one,
They have an Everest,
It cannot be moved.
Be sure to follow Jesus,
It's a mammoth step.
So much to clear away,
Stacks of habits,

Wrong thoughts,
Wrong actions,
Wrong company.
So much to overcome.
A heap of mountains !
And you can win with Jesus.
Your mountains will be moved !
Life changes.
You and Jesus,
You come together,
Thank Him for all the help,
It happens,
Time and time again.
Hallelujah !

MY SUPERMAN

There is only one Superman.
Jesus Christ our Saviour.
Thank God for Jesus !
For three years
He walked through Galilee.
He preached love,
He healed the sick.
In the synagogue
He bravely spoke the truth.
In His travels
He mixed with everyone.
Religious leaders,
Lepers,
Tax collectors,
Even prostitutes.
Crowds followed Him everywhere.

He was always in danger.
Enemies made plots.
Jesus knew the final outcome.
Like a Superman supreme
He faced His enemies,
Endured humiliation,
Terrific pain
And still showed love.
No one could do the same.
And Jesus rose from the dead
Superman supreme.
He lives !
He is our Superman,
He is so much more.
Hallelujah !

NEVER WALK ALONE

We all have times,
Times of loneliness,
Times of trouble,
Even nightmares.
In all such times
We need friends.
Friends to comfort,
Friends to advise,
To walk your road.
So many do not know,
Do not believe
That they have a great friend.
One who is always present.
Simply said,
It's Jesus your Saviour.
He is literally your Saviour,

Your Redeemer.
He loves you deeply.
Learn the old phrase,
"Walk and talk with Jesus".
Do it always,
Not just with troubles,
Always each day.
Your constant companion.
It's the answer,
Trust Him,
Have faith,
Be faithful,
Truly believe.
You'll never walk alone.
Hallelujah !

NEVER TOO YOUNG

Knowing Jesus,
It's for every age.
You are never too young.
He loved you from the start.
Whatever age,
There is no barrier.
He wants you,
The earlier the better !
Jesus needs you,
Needs you to follow.
Jesus said,
"Let the children come to me".
The same goes for teenagers.
Each of you,
You are very important.
Never think you do not count.
Never think you have to wait.

Show your elders,
Show them you can be active,
Show them you can fish,
Show them an example.
Teenagers,
You bring your mates.
Be steadfast,
Prove to your friends,
Prove being a Christian is tops.
Show the Jesus Way.
It's for them,
It's for every one.
Pray for your friends,
Lead them your way.
The Lord is with you,
Keep close to Jesus.
Hallelujah !

NO LUCK

So many talk of luck!
What rubbish !
There is no such thing !
Bad luck does not exist.
Neither does good luck.
It's a man-made superstition.
Luck is like an idol.
Millions follow it !
See the long lottery queues !
See the crowds at races.
Pagan pursuits.
Worshipping a pagan god.
Lady luck, she is unreal.
People live for jackpots.
Money wasted.
It can be addictive.
Addicted to gambling.

The Bible spurns luck.
It leads into sin.
We are taught to strive,
Strive honestly.
Use our lives for God,
Win through,
Earn our entry,
Our entry to eternal life.
There is no luck in this.
We are wrapped in love,
In cheerful service,
With dedication.
Erase the thought of luck,
You'll never need it,
You have God.
Hallelujah !

NO POCKETS IN A SHROUD

It's an old Spanish saying.
No pockets in a shroud.
Too true !
There are none !
Yet we need reminding !
Life is eternal,
Riches are not.
Live close to God,
Happily practical.
Enjoy life on earth,
Enjoy the Godly way.
Build up spiritual riches.
Such riches last forever.

Live as if heaven is on earth !
Enjoy what you do.
Walk with Jesus,
Never leave Him.
Let your being shine.
Shine with Holy happiness.
Reflect God's glory,
Share your joy.
Spread your spiritual wealth,
Share the riches with others,
Make lives worthwhile,
For you are rich !
Hallelujah !

NO SECRETS

Be sure that you know,
All your thoughts,
All your plans,
All you say and do,
All are known by God.
Every selfish deed,
Any lustful thoughts,
He knows.
There are no secrets,
Nothing can be hidden.
You must know this.
Indeed, it is good to know!
It helps the way we live,
It gives us a will,

A will to live well.
It puts a brake on evil,
It encourages sincerity,
Dedication,
Concentration.
We come closer to God.
No skeletons in cupboards !
All is confessed to God,
And God forgives us.
Let us be very thankful,
Lets us love wholly,
We are His !
Hallelujah !

NO WAY BORING !

It's been said by many,
"Christians are boring !"
Some are !
Avoid them !
They are dead wrong !
They are ignorant of joy.
Are we mostly boring ?
Never !
Real Christians
Real ones,
They are full of joy.
Full of action,
Full of enthusiasm,
No time to be bored,
No time to be boring !
Being a Christian,
It's unbeatable !
Out of the secular world !
It's the sharing of happiness,

Incomparable Christian fellowship.
It is a new world.
A world of love,
A world of assurance,
A world of stability
And most of all,
It leads to eternal life.
Life in the heavenly Kingdom.
Boring ?
Not even for an hour |!
If you are a doubter
Come in for a treat !
You're invited now,
Join in,
Belong to Jesus,
Be with Jesus,
Right now !
Hallelujah !

NOW! NOW! NOW!

This is urgent !
Very urgent !
The call to repent.
It comes from Jesus.
Repent sounds old fashioned !
Just be sorry,
Really sorry !
Being Christians
It's the biggest step you make.
It's life changing.
There is nothing greater,
Do not chicken out !
It's stupid,
Stupid to ignore this call.
It's you to choose.
Choose between heaven and hell.
Between a great lasting life
And a life that is useless.
Know Jesus,
Do not ignore Him,
He died for you,
You'd better believe it !
Do not hang about,

You know full well
Christians are with Jesus.
You know you should be there!
Delaying shows unbelief,
That shows a sinful way.
Take the challenge,
Act on it now.
Now is the time,
Now is your chance,
Now is the call.
Give your all,
Every bit of yourself,
Walk into happiness,
Walk into eternal life,
Experience God's peace.
Let your life shine,
Shine on others,
Make a difference to ourself,
A difference to others.
Now! Now!Now!
It is your future,
Hallelujah !

OLD AGE BLUES

Many churches,
Most members are elderly.
People with good service,
Served in Sunday School,
Served in fellowships,
In Bible Classes
And in other ways.
Age has caught up with them.
They have slowed down.
Possibly retired.
But that is not right!
In The Bible
There is no retirement !
God waits for them,
Waits for action !
Join an old folks group,
Take Jesus with you,
Show His love,

Be an example,
Win their respect.
Then talk of Jesus,
Talk of your church,
Invite some to attend.
Accompany them.
Sit with them in church.
Service in old age,
God wants you,
It's a challenge.
Think of other ways.
Befriend people,
Show the Jesus Way,
Never give up.
Don't retire,
You are needed.
Hallelujah !

OLD TEMPTATIONS

So many believe in nothing !
They never think of God,
Nor do they believe in the devil !
They live for themselves,
For nothing else.
Get to know such people.
Try and befriend them.
Find the right time,
The time to ask a question,
One that leads to Jesus.
"What do you think of God"
Or "Ever been to church ?".
They are openings.
They need to know of Jesus,
Of Christians,
Of active churches.
Keep on about your Saviour.
Talk of a new life.

Explain about sin,
About temptations.
That all have temptations,
That they come from the devil,
And tell that the devil is real.
That Jesus was tempted.
How Christians beat the devil.
How Christians speak to Jesus,
How Christians know their future.
Never give up,
Lead through prayer,
Some may deny Christ,
Others you will win.
God is with you,
With you always.
Just thank Him.
Hallelujah !

ON FIRE !

I cannot keep quiet !
I will not keep quiet.
I've got the greatest gift,
I've got Jesus,
Jesus my Saviour.
And He has got me !
It's incredible !
It's astounding !
Me with Jesus !
I'm not worthy,
I am a sinner,
That's what makes it so great !
I've been converted,
I've been conquered !
Now I cannot keep still !
I cannot be idle,
I have to share Jesus.
One thing I cannot understand,
I cannot understand the idle,

The idle Christians.
They are so different !
Jesus is in me,
He's all around me.
I've got spiritual stamina,
He's made me glow !
I'm on fire for Jesus !
Just think !
If all Christians caught fire !
The church would change,
The town would change,
The world would change !
Be ready for Revival !
Burst into flame,
Let your flame spread,
Let no one put it out !
Spread the fire,
Spread the Gospel News'
Hallelujah !

ONLY GOD

Only God !
What do you mean ?
It means everything !
Each day,
Even each hour
We stand for God.
Whatever we do
All should be
All for God.
How we think,
What we do,
What we say,
All in Godly ways.
Sounds hard ?
It is not !
It's a real fact,
It makes your life,

Makes it worthwhile.
You'll never feel alone,
Jesus is with you.
It is a privilege,
A privilege for believers.
You are hand in hand
Walking with Jesus.
You'll still have troubles,
Still have obstacles
But your prayers,
Your faith,
Help clear the way.
Reading God's Word.
So much help,
So much assurance.
His Word the energy source.
Hallelujah

ON THE CREST OF A WAVE

There is nothing better,
Almost indescribable,
Way beyond anything else,
Knowing Jesus !
Nothing greater !
It has to be shared.
He is for all !
Stir up our families,
Move to our friends,
Find more opportunities,
Times to share with all.
Do not shirk,
Do not be selfish,
Jesus must be shared.
He told us this,
To go out in the world,

Our little world,
Anywhere
And tell the Good News.
On the crest of a wave ?
Keep up there !
Pull up others,
Others to love the Lord.
It's like on a mountain top,
It's "Cloud Nine"
So share it !
Keep on keeping on,
Along God's eternal road.
Enjoy it !
God wants this.
Sing out your thanks !
Hallelujah !

OTHERS

Who comes first ?
Usually you do !
Who rarely comes first ?
Jesus !
We were born selfish,
From child to teenager,
And then to adult,
Selfish.
Me! Me! Me!,
It can go on that way -
Unless …
Unless you follow Jesus.
Knowing Jesus,
Being born again.
So many things to change.

Out goes selfishness.
Jesus teaches us,
How to love,
How to care,
How to go the second mile,
How not to count the cost.
No more just you.
It means no more greed,
Putting others first
And you are happy !
Smiles not frowns,
Eagerness !
Friends with all.
It is a blessing !
Hallelujah !

OUT OF STEP

Loving Jesus,
We are out of step.
Moving against the tide.
We are different.
We do not fit in.
Some say we are strange !
Maybe so to some.
There is a good reason,
We strive to be "Little Christs".
It's a hard target,
Very hard.
It takes every spiritual ounce !
Following Jesus,
Not just a phrase,
A life of dedication.
A life to be obedient.
Loving Jesus is great

So we do our very best.
So many ways to be active,
Almost unending.
Yes, we are different,
Joyously different,
Humbly different.
Yes out of step,
Thankfully out of step.
We pray for the day,
The day when steps will change,
When more and more come in,
Following Jesus.
For the day we will all be the same,
All in step,
In step with Jesus.
May His will be done.
Hallelujah !

OUT OF THIS WORLD

Out of this world
Yet still in it !
Out of the secular,
Out of the sordid
Out of the tawdry
Into real life.
Through changing worlds
To a spirit filled world.
The world with Jesus.
His spiritual world,
It goes to eternal life.
Serving Jesus,
Forgetting yourself,
Just sharing Jesus.
Loving others
That's the Jesus World !
Be sure to be in it !

The greatest change in life.
Completely wonderful.
You look around,
You look with new eyes,
You listen,
Listen with new ears,
You think,
Think with a changed mind.
You are dedicated.
You aim to save others,
To give them the joy,
The joy of following Jesus.
Live this life,
Live it in every way,
There is nothing better.
Hallelujah !

PAGAN PEOPLE

Pagan people,
You know so many.
Our Western lands
They are pagan.
Government leaders,
They never reflect God's glory.
They never point the way.
All levels of life
They are so secular.
So much crime,
So much fear,
Riots and strikes,
There is no peace.
A world awash in sin.
But do not be dismayed !
In spite of everything
The Lord reigns.
He made the earth,
He created us all,

His will will be done.
Believe in Him,
Believe totally,
Show your colours,
Do not be afraid.
Fight pagan ways,
Show how love wins through.
We know,
No doubt at all
That God is victorious.
This is His world,
It always will be.
Rejoice !
Fight through the gloom,
Lighten the darkness,
God's light is strong,
Shine with His glory.
All will be well !
Hallelujah !

PASSPORTS

In the long run
There are two passports,
One for Heaven
One for Hell !
Some would laugh at this !
Scornfully walk on.
Remember Noah !
He built an ark,
People laughed at him !
They thought him mad.
And they drowned.
It's the same right now.
Laughing about Heaven and Hell.
Settle down !
Believe – one way or the other.
Be sensible !
Take the heavenly way.

It's free !
For all who follow Jesus.
The devoted,
The dedicated,
Those born again.
For all who serve Jesus,
All who are spiritually active.
There are no exclusions.
Bring people to Christ,
Ensure they have passports.
Lead the way to worship,
Lead the way to Jesus.
It is your ministry.
Go flat out to save,
Flat out to rescue,
Never give up !
Hallelujah !

PONDER LONGER

How much time is spent,
Spent daily with the Lord ?
Is it in minutes,
Or in hours ?
We all must read His Word,
We all must pray and pray.
And when you pray
Pray as friend to friend.
Pray as if he is your Father.
That means listening as well !
One way praying
It is unreal.
Talking to a friends,
You also listen.
Do so in prayer.
Ponder.
We need a measure of meditation.
Time to think on Jesus.
Time to picture His Ministry.
Time for prayerful thoughts.

Thoughts that may come from Jesus.
You just have to make that space,
Coming closer, much closer.
Someone said,
"Use your common-sense" -
It may be a Jesus way.
Be assured,
He will lead,
Lead in His time,
In His Way.
You need that time,
That time to ponder,
Precious periods.
Ponder longer.
The more you do so
The more you will be led.
Follow this way,
It is His Way
Hallelujah !

PRAY-AS-YOU-GO

Yes, pray always.
It starts the day,
You cannot pray too much !
You are talking to God.
Aim at something hourly..
Pray for all sorts.
Passing a church ?
Pray for it.
In the shop?
Pray for the people.
Pass a betting shop ?
Pray for the punters.
See a policeman ?
They need prayer.
See children playing ?
Then pray for them.

You are walking with Jesus,
Learn to love people.
As you go along,
You see see beauty,
Give thanks,
Thanks to your Creator.
Thinking of loved ones ?
Thank Him again.
Feel you've missed a task
Room for forgiveness !
Pray as you go,
Wherever you go.
It makes your day,
You are never alone.
What a privilege !
Hallelujah !

PRAYING CHURCHES

Every church and chapel,
All have prayers.
But are they praying churches ?
Or are prayers a little weak,
Mostly from the pulpit ?
Are they just on Sundays ?
Way back
Every church,
Every chapel
They had weekly prayer meetings.
Member after member
Showing prayerful inspiration.
Prayers of joy,
Prayer of thanksgiving,
Pleading prayers,
Planning prayers.
So many praying,
Praying from the heart.
Prayers on fire
And the pray-ers as well.

And God will respond.
Far too often now
There are no such meetings.
Enthusiasm is dead.
Who is to blame ?
It's everyone !
Pastors and members.
This must change !
Start again
Even with two or three.
Through prayer more will join,
Sparks start a fire.
Your church will be alive again.
The more prayer-filled
The greater the church.
The greater the result.
Become prayer-conditioned
It leads to miracles !
Hallelujah !

PREACHING THE WORD

Every Sunday
In every church
God's Word is preached.
Dedicated preachers
Preaching.
But far too often
Those sermons are forgotten.
Forgotten by Monday !
Why ?
Often there is no challenge,
There is nothing,
Nothing to remember !
Sermons must have a message,
One that sticks.
Preferably pointing to action.
All from God's Words.

God's commands,
Commands to be obeyed.
Sermons should show comfort,
Show reassurance,
Showing God's Way.
Stirring the listener,
Helping to bring enthusiasm.
For dedicated service.
Sermons to remember,
Sermons for taking notes.
Worthwhile sermons.
Effectual and lasting
Just as Jesus preached.
Pray for this,
Rely on the Lord.
Hallelujah !

PROVE GOD !

Prove God !
"Impossible !" some say.
They must be blind !
Deaf as well !
Walk in a forest.
Who grew the trees ?
Hear the bird song,
Who made them sing ?
Pick a flower,
Who made it ?
Can men do these things ?
No way !
It's God's Creation
All the way.
Forget cities,
Forget man made places.
Stand still,

Feel the silence !
Another Godly gift.
Creation ?
Every iota !
You ?
Same again !.
Not to believe,
It shows a little mind !
Even so God made it,
Spoilt by the owner !
Think deeply,
You must know,
Must know God is the answer.
All good things come from God.
It is His Creation
Thank the Lord !
Hallelujah !

PULL NO PUNCHES !

It's this way,
Deciding on your life,
Which way to go,
How to cope with your life.
Too many are too polite,
Too timid,
Afraid to be blunt !
They know the way,
They know Christ,
Yet they fail to tell,
Tell the basic facts.
Stress these :
Jeus loves you utterly,
Accept Him as Saviour,
It is a "must" for all.
Do not omit other facts,
Some find it too scary.
Scared to tell the alternative.

The Bible clearly states
Hundreds of times,
Those who reject Jesus
They have eternal life,
Eternal life in Hell.
It's a choice,
A choice of a great future
Or a doomed future.
Tell this with care,
No fire or brimstone,
Tell it lovingly,
Let them know
They are wanted,
Wanted by Jesus.
Stress He calls them,
But keep to the truth.
Hallelujah !

READ THAT BOOK !

Read The Bible,
Read all of it,
All of it every year !
God's Words to you.
From Creation,
Through the prophets,
Christ's birth,
His suffering,
His death,
His resurrection
His messages of love,
His last days.
The lives of the Apostles,
Paul's adventures.
Never, never, never
Shut your Bible !
His Word to you,

His Word to all.
The Bible is Holy,
The Bible is sacred,
It's also dynamite !
It has changed billions.
It will change the world..
Read it well,
Mark it well,
Find the hidden gems,
It is a treasure trove.
Share His Word,
Carry it with you,
Use it well.
Thank God for His Way,
The Book of His love.
Hallelujah !

REBEL WITH A CAUSE

Stand with out fear,
You are special !
Stand out like a sore thumb !
Why ?
Because you are a rebel !
You've accepted Jesus,
He is your Saviour.
You've made the break,
You've left the old worldly ways,
You've left the crowd.
It was a great decision,
Now Jesus is close.
Do as He tells you,
Go out and fish,
Fish for souls.
Don't be static !
Do not be a pew sitter.
You are led by God,
Led by His commands.
Stand firm,
Stand out,

You are on duty,
On duty all the time.
Be on the move with Jesus,
Be very different.
You'll lose friends,
And gain far more !
Too often you find Christians,
Christians only in name.
Love them
But do not copy them !
Love them into action !
You may be lonely,
It will not stay that way,
Wake up your Church !
Your example will be seen.
Seen and more will follow.
Just be different
Different for Christ,
Enjoy it !
Hallelujah !

RELIGIOUS TREADMILL

Too many Christians
They are on a treadmill !
Sunday going to church,
Weekdays mostly idle.
Maybe one meeting
Maybe a social event.
Then Sunday again.
A boring treadmill.
What is missing ?
A seven day Godly week.
They need to obey the Holy Spirit.
Following Gospel commands,
Living every day with Jesus.
Only too often -
Far too often
The church is to blame.
No teaching for eagerness,
For enthusiasm.

No special aims,
No targets.
No move to evangelise.
No weekly prayer meetings.
It's a mechanical church,
Maybe a comfortable church.
Not even cell meetings.
Churches with no mission.
Change it !
Rebel !
Rebel against a sleepy church.
Awake the members,
Bring them to life,
Seven days a week.
What a change !
What joy !
Hallelujah !

RETIREMENT

Growing older ?
Planning retirement ?
No more commuting,
No more bosses,
No more stress !
A feet-up paradise !
You're right and wrong !
There is no retirement,
None at all in The Bible !
For Christians it's like this,
You'll have a life change.
But you must still be active,
Active for Jesus.
Be fully dedicated,
Be happy to serve
Now you have more time,
Time to be useful.
Use it for the Lord,

Do so gladly.
Visitation,
Leading a prayer group,
Supporting your Pastor
And whatever is needed.
It fills your life,
Fills it wonderfully.
Far better than feet-up!
Bring more to your Church,
So much is possible.
Retirement ?
No way,
You have a new ministry,
Life is being full-filled"
Keep on going,
Keep on for Jesus,
Hallelujah !

RIPPLE EFFECT

Throw a stone in a pool,
Watch the ripple effect.
You made those ripples.
The same goes with your life.
Stand still, do nothing
Nothing happens.
Do something,
Something happens.
Those ripples.
Serving the Lord,
Your ripples begin.
We can never be sure,
Never be sure of results,
The Lord decides.
Your ripples spread,

The greater the effort,
Greater are the ripples.
Imagine,
Every Christian in action !
Widening ripples,
The world would change !
All in a life time.
Give more ripples to Him,
There is no limit.
One day you will know,
Know what the ripples did.
Keep at it,
Enjoy it !
Hallelujah !

ROBOT FACES

Walk down the high street,
Go through any crowd.
What do you see ?
Robot faces !
Young ones,
Old ones.
Mostly somewhat glum.
Or expressionless.
A few look thoughtful,
One or two may smile.
Aimless faces,
Almost lifeless.
If you are a Christian -
Smile, keep smiling.

Walk with joyful thoughts,
Smile at others,
And pray as you walk.
Then, if in a queue,
Talk and smile.
Be positive in what you say,
You may even plant seeds.
Godly seeds.
Carry invitations for your church.
Use them with prayer.
You'll walk with lighter steps,
You're walking with Jesus.
Hallelujah !

SAINTS ALIVE !

Saints alive !
Yes, many are !
Surprisingly.
Seemingly ordinary people.
They are found in churches,
In village chapels,
Any denomination.
Elderly saints
Quietly serving the Lord.
Probably for many years.
All kinds of ministries.
Church cleaners,
Brass polishers,
Sunday school teachers,
Choir members,
Lay preachers
And much more.

Totally dedicated.
Toiling gladly.
Often taken for granted,
They do not expect praise.
They just love the Lord,
Love their Church,
Love their work.
No one calls them saints,
They would deny such a name.
People who know,
Who look outwards,
They see them as saints.
Examples from the Jesus Team.
Never counting the cost.
Thank the Lord !
Hallelujah !

SAND CASTLES

Sand castles on the beach.
Made beautifully,
Turrets,
A drawbridge,
Flags.
Proudly made.
Then the tide comes in,
The castle crumbles.
It disappears.
Not even a trace.
It can happen to you !
With your life
Unless you follow Jesus.
You build your own kingdom,
You have a house,
A car,
A garden,
Maybe a caravan,
Maybe a lake chalet.
Possibly a good bank balance.

Makes you feel good,
You feel comfortable.
But Christians know,
Know all is temporary.
All those things
Just for life on earth.
It's time to prepare,
Prepare for God's Kingdom.
Eternal life,
It is forever,
Far more value,
Far greater.
Worldly wealth,
Worldly comforts, fair enough !
But Godly wealth
Your life investment.
Live for that,
Be positively happy.
Hallelujah !

SEE A NEED MEET IT

One inspired church,
It has a motto,
"See a need, meet it".
We should all use this.
Adopt it for yourselves.
See a need meet it.
Just as Jesus did !
Jesus did this,
With the sick and lame,
With the blind,
With the bereaved,
With the hungry.
Done for all.
Follow this,
It shows your love,

It reflects your faith.
It is a witness,
Putting others first.
No task is too low,
No need to be menial,
Serving Jesus
That makes the difference.
Think of all you do,
Think of them as heavenly tasks,
God's love.
Show this to those you help,
Actions speaks.
Meet those needs,
The Lord is with you.
Hallelujah !

SECULAR SICKNESS

Go into any street,
Look at the people,
Pale faces,
Sad faces,
Not many with a smile.
Painted faces,
Embedded rings.
People in a hurry
And God loves them all.
Trouble is,
Most suffer secular sickness.
They seem soul-less.
Many brought up without God,
Ignorant of God's love.
Others who knew better,
Overcome by Satan.
Young pagans,

Nobody told them anything.
Not their fault.
What can be done ?
Send out a red alert.
Alert every Christian !
Every Church member.
Instil inspiration,
Appeal to their beliefs.
It starts with prayer,
It goes to planned outreach.
Consecrated aims.
The tide can be turned,
Turned with God's help.
God is in charge.
Follow Him in every way.
Hallelujah !

SHOWERS OF BLESSING

Many of us,
We take things for granted.
We fail to be thankful.
Who to ?
The Lord of course !
Look back,
Be honest !
When you got a job,
If you became betrothed,
If you passed exams,
When recovered from illness
Did you thank the Lord ?
All and more
All showers of blessing.
Be fully aware,
All good things,
They come from God.

Sometimes we remember,
More often we do not.
Look back again.
The time you made a friend,
That wonderful vacation,
An inspiring meeting,
A good Church Service,
An enjoyable walk,
Do some thanking !
Get praising.
The Lord has provided.
Thank Him !
His gifts are so great,
It makes for happiness.
You are truly blessed !
Hallelujah !

SHARP OR BLUNT ?

Even sharp knives go blunt.
They have to be honed.
Then tested.
Those who love Jesus,
Who serve Jesus,
We can tire,
We can get frustrated.
In other words,
Eagerness gets blunted.
These are the times
We need to be revived.
Our wits need sharpening.
Maybe a spritual Retreat
Or a weekend of prayer.
A spiritual break
For us and the Lord,
He will invigorate us.

He will lead us.
Pastors and members
All need refreshing.
Churches can get stale,
They need honing sometimes.
Sharpen with Revival ways,
Look for new outreach.
Instil enthusiasm,
Enthusiasm for every member.
Aim for excitement,
Aim for eagerness,
Bring in expectation.
Churches coming to life !
Members fully alive !
Time to move ahead,
To stay ahead !
Hallelujah !

SHRINK THE IDOLS

We don't have idols,
We are Christians !
Dear friends, you are wrong !
Look at your lives !
You men,
What do you do :
With your car,
With a hobby,
Playing golf,
Watching sports ?
Dear ladies how about you ?
Home beautification ?
Gardening ?
Socialising ?
Shopping ?
Nothing wrong in those !
But check the hours,

Hours for each pursuit.
Then how much time with Jesus ?
With serving Him.
Which has priority ?
We may not mean to slack,
To overshadow our Saviour.
Too often we do have idols,
Pursuits that take over.
Live a varied life,
Enjoy your pastimes,
But put Jesus first !
Serving Jesus,
It is enjoyable,
It is invigorating
So have a really varied life,
A happy life.
Hallelujah !

SINGING LIES !

We love singing hymns,
Praising the Lord.
Wonder words,
Comfortable words,
Music to warm the heart.
Hold on though !
Too often we sing and sing,
Sing without thought !
Do we mean what we sing ?
Hymns as these :
"I'd rather have Jesus
Than silver or gold".
Do we really mean it ?
Some will, some will not.
Or when we sing,
"Jesus guides us o'er the tumult".
Do we answer the call ?

Or is it just a song ?
Dozens and dozens of hymns,
Calling for action.
Hymns soaked in meanings.
Take care !
Sing what you mean !
No more singing lies !
We do not mean to lie,
We just need more thought.
Be honest.
Even be silent on some lines !
Thank the Lord for hymns,
For the writers,
For the joy of singing.
Sing truly
It's far more fun !
Hallelujah !

SLIPPING BACK

Following Jesus,
We do not turn back.
We gave up our old ways,
Gave them up for good.
However most of us slip.
Even if not seen,
All are imperfect !
Sometimes
We fail to mirror Christ.
Some become pew sitters
They've lost their zeal.
Slip to trivial things
Then forgetting their Lord.
They become Sunday people,
Some in time,
They drop out.
So sad,
Sad for Jesus,
Sad for the drop outs.
It need not happen.
Direct contact,

Member to member.
It's a kind of buddy system
Each cares for the other.
The stronger ones
They support the weaker ones.
Serving Christ,
Keeping the faith.
Each member
Lean over backward
Strive never to lose anyone.
Real Christ-led fellowship.
Then each pair,
Go for fishing !
What an adventure !
Think of your church,
Think all are a family.
Family in Christ.
Now add to your family !
Praise the Lord,
Hallelujah !

SO CLOSE

He knows you,
Inside out !
Doubt it ?
Read Psalm 40.
No way can you hide.
He knows what you'll say,
What you think,
He knows your dreams.
Scary ?
Not if you love Him.
It is reassuring !
Just think !
God your Father knows you !
So get to know Him !
Read well His Words.

Pray carefully,
Meaningful prayers,
Spend time listening.
Realise The Holy Spirit,
He is within you.
Realise God's closeness,
Within.
He's part of you !
Rejoice and be glad,
Thank Him !
You were born again,
You have that new life,
So close,
So live it !
Hallelujah !

SO WHAT ?

So what ?
What's so good ?
Being a Christian ?
What's wrong with parties ?
What's wrong with sex ?
With swearing ?
Christians must be boring !
Bored rotten !
Stiff-necked !
Too good for anyone !
Just hold it my friend.
I've listened,
It's my turn now !
Bored ? No way.
No time for that.
We are over the moon !
Too good ?
No way !
No one can be that good !
Stiff-necked ?
We're too happy !

Partying ?
We do that !
Too much fun to use alcohol.
Why spoil your body ?
Why waste cash ?
Sex is God-given,
Use it God's way.
Swearing is blasphemy,
Why belittle God ?
That is a no- no always.
God made you,
God sent His Son,
To show you the way.
You're missing out,
Missing on Cloud Nine.
Come on in,
Know the Lord,
You'll find out !
Get born again,
Know the joy !
Hallelujah !

STAR GAZING

Go outside,
On a clear night.
Look at the stars,
Keep looking,
The more you look
The more incredible !
Worlds apart.
A universal unending scene,
Stars,planets,comets.
They are countless,
They are beyond our knowledge,
Sheer proof of God !
Man cannot compete.
All were created,
By God of course !
The sun,

The moon,
All those stars,
All in place,
Exactly so.
Moved slightly
The world could end.
God rules the Universe.
His wonders so great.
Look at those stars !,
Keep looking,
Get that feel,
The feel of Almighty God !
Worship Him,
Love Him,
Serve Him !
Hallelujah !

STORMY WEATHER

Life as a Christians
Never a smooth ride.
Believers, Unbelievers,
All have ups and downs.
All go through stormy weather.
Dark valleys.
Some will slip and fall.
But Christians have help,
God is with us,
Every hour,
Every day,
Every week,
At all times night and day.
Dark valleys don't last,
God's light is with us.
Troubles and problems,
They toughen us.

We have faith,
We have the Lord,
His love shines out.
Do not fear,
Pray often,
Listen often.
With God-filled happiness,
Christians thrive,
Ready to help others
Ready to lighten their loads.
Storms never last
And they will be followed by peace.
Spiritual quiet.
Calmness.
Appreciate the rough,
Rejoice in the smooth.
Hallelujah !

STUCK IN THE MUD

It's happened to most.
We've gone through mud,
We've got stuck
With great effort
We pull free.
Or with help from others.
In life we can get stuck.
We cannot advance,
Sometimes we stay put,
We stagnate.
We are not capable
Just by ourselves,
Help is needed.
Realise this.
Spiritually we often get stuck.

Pride steps in,
Bad habits hold us.
Don't be too independent,
Pray for help !
Walk with Jesus
He'll pull you through.
Static Christians
They are not blessed.
Walk with Jesus,
Do not stay behind.
Know Him,
Know Him as your friend,
Feel His Presence,
Keep right in touch !
Hallelujah !

STUMBLING

A lot of us stumble,
Stumble on the Jesus journey.
There is usually a reason.
The devil may have tripped you.
It's not an excuse,
You played your part.
When we stumble
Go straight to prayer,
Be determined,
Do not give up !
One wise person said,
Fall down seven times,
Get up eight times!".
Jesus told us,
"No man is perfect".

He knows we can stumble.
Even so,
Make no excuses.
We must face problems,
We must aim to win.
Help others who fall,
Pick them up with love.
Back onto an even keel.
It's team work,
You,others and Jesus.
The Lord is with you – Get up !
Carry on !
He loves you.
Hallelujah !

SURFACE ONLY !

Go to almost any church,
Sadly all have them,
Surface Christians !
They are always there,
In that respect,
They are loyal,
They are counted.
But scrape the surface,
Somewhat shallow.
What do they do ?
Almost nothing !
Sometimes they are faultless,
They have been neglected,
Talents never used.
The church has failed them.
Others, they are contented,
Contented to just sit.
It is a sacred duty,

Stirring all to serve,
Stopping stagnation.
Aim for every Christian,
Every one to have a ministry.
The Bible says,
"All are priests" to have ministries.
Kindle enthusiasm,
Stoke it up !
Boost the urge to serve,
For all be second milers.
You can make the difference.
It's having your church
Born again !
New life for your church,
Empty pews filled.
Surface Christians ?
No more, no longer !
Hallelujah !

SWIM AGAINST THE TIDE ?

Can you swim ?
Have you ever swum
Against the tide ?
It can be tough,
Headway is slow.
It takes all your energy.
Just like that,
As hard as that,
Is being an active Christian.
It needs stamina,
Lots of faith-
And Jesus to help.
There will some friends,
Some who keep away.
Old temptations to fight,

Old habits to reject,
Fighting with Satan.
Be thankful,
Thankful for Jesus' help.
Every day is special,
And every day to God's Way.
The harder the day
The tougher you become.
It helps,
You get stronger,
You are better equipped.
You are a great example,
A little Christ,
Part of the Jesus Team.
Hallelujah !

TEEN AGE CHAMPS

Teenagers,
You are priority peop[e,
You are future leaders,
You will be the Church.
Prepare yourselves.
Be sure you know Jesus,
Strive to get closer,
Pray for direction.
Be guided,
Think about your church,
What needs to be done ?
Especially for teenagers.
Don't hang about,
Serving Jesus non-stop.
Never leave things for others.
You have enthusiasm ?

If not you fail !
Infect older members,
They may be battle weary,
Or need a push.
Be a challenger,
Stir your church !
Show what you can do.
It's tough as a teenager,
Prove you can cope.
Work out your tasks,
We call them ministries.
Fish for more teenagers,
Run challenging events,
It is an adventure,
And Jesus supports you.
Hallelujah !

THANK GOD !

Often we pray,
Pray one sided prayers.
Some like a grocery list.
A wish list.
Go for real prayer !
Thank you prayers !
We take too much for granted !
Remember this,
All good things come from God.
Never take them for granted.
Thank God every day
For your daily life,
For health,
For home and family,
For friends,

For problems solved.
Been out ?
Thank Him for a safe journey,
For food,
For security
And events as they come.
Write a thanking list !
Most of all,
Thank God for Jesus !
For Jesus' great sacrifice,
His wonderful love.
Make every day
A thanksgiving day.
Happily thankful.
Hallelujah !

THE "A" TEAM

Within your church
Start an "A" Team !
Enthusiastic people
Dedicated people.
Plan your tasks,
Visiting the lonely,
Helping the elderly,
Working with youth.
Sounds a big order ?
Not if shared.
It's a challenge,
It's an adventure,
It's serving God.
He helps you all the way.
The "A" Team starts with prayer,
Never work without it.

Enjoy the tasks,
Talk oof Jesus when you call,
Pray with those you meet.
Be privileged in your tasks,
Cleaning jobs,
Digging a garden,
Shopping,
Cooking,
Writing letters,
All done for Jesus !
Keep the plans going,
Think of new ones,
It's love unlimited.
Start your "A" Team,
Start it now !
Hallelujah !

THE DOOLITTLE FAMILY

They are a good family,
Regular at church,
Living honestly,
But they do little,
Almost nothing !
Attending Sunday Service,
Nothing else.
At home a dusty Bible.
Seemingly a dull life.
No thought of action !
Then there was a change,
A new Church leader,
A new broom.
A man on fire for Christ.
His sermons point the way

All to serve their Saviour !
Help on fishing for souls,
Help to start cells.
All are seen,
All encouraged.
Every member challenged,
To meet their neighbours.
To invite friends to fellowship,
To church.
Prayer meetings for all,
Enthusiasm spreads.
The church comes alive !
With action and love.
The birth of new lives.
Hallelujah !

D.I.Y BOOK

The "Do it yourself Book".
The best Book in the world,
World best seller.
The Holy Bible.
And Holy it is !
Written for you and for me.
Use it !
Do what it tells you !
Really read it.
It's bursting with life
It tells you how to live,
It tells you what to do,
It tells you about friends,
It tells you about God,
About His Son Jesus,
About the Holy Spirit,
And so much more.
Mark down key verses.

Don't be put off.
With history,
With family trees,
With rituals.
It is so valuable,
A life saver !.
Focussing on love,
On you and on me.
It is incomparable,
Your cup will run over !
Genesis to Revelations
Gems in every book.
Get into it !
Discuss it,
Know it really well.
God's Word for you !
Hallelujah !

THE DYING CHURCH

It is only too common,
Just a handful of people
Every Sunday.
Mostly empty pews,
Mostly elderly folk,
Often no children,
Few if any teenagers.
Those that attend,
They are lovingly loyal,
Their memories,
Of crowded Sunday Schools,
Well filled churches,
Busy weekday meetings.
A choir.
And now a dying chapel.
What can be done ?
Send a plea for help.

Help from a stronger church.
A few dedicated workers,
To help for a year or more.
Busy with visitation,
Each with a church member.
Busy planning mid week events,
Publicising them.
Every action prayer-covered.
Chapels and churches,
They can be saved.
The choice is do or die.
It is commonsense,
It is a sacred ministry,
It is saving lives
And God's House is saved.
Hallelujah !

"THIS IS THE NEWS"

We hear the media every day.
News of unrest,
Of murders, divorces, death.
Of recession,
Of inflation,
All gloomy news.
Rarely anything positive.
The secular world.
Even so there is good news,
Unpublished good news.
Secular media ignore it.
News of people,
People who help people,
Of happy events,
News of healing,
News of good deeds
And lots more.
The greatest news,

Ignored by most,
Jesus is alive !
Jesus loves each person.
That millions are born again.
Not a word in the media !
A good example -
In China
Thousands a day
They come to Christ.
Of churches overflowing
And Christian ministries.
The Gospel News,
Be part of it,
You'll never be famous,
Just a humble little Christ.
Be excited,
Eternal life is yours !
Hallelujah !

TONGUE TIED

Are you an extrovert
Or are you an introvert ?
Able to talk a donkey's leg off,
Or tongue tied ?
Almost speechless !
Either way God needs you.
Prepare to be used !
The talker can use the tongue,
The tongue in God's work.
A mighty weapon wisely used.
He can preach, he can witness.
The quiet one,
Just as valuable.
He or she God will lead.
With prayer,
Nervousness will lessen,
Eagerness will take over.

Actions can speak
Speak where words did not.
Such people radiate love,
The second mile often walked.
It's a real adventure.
Nothing is too much.
It is the Jesus Way.
Never belittle yourself,
God leads you.
You are in God's Plan.
You are important.
Never doubt,
Never give up.
Never lose faith,
You are in His Family.
Hallelujah !

TREADMILLS

Ever been on a treadmill ?
It's a nonstop moving belt.
You walk or run on it.
It's good exercise,
Some spend hours on it.
Just one thing,
It gets you nowhere !
Life for most is the same.
We live and live and live,
Often purposelessly.
It can be soul destroying,
Day after day
With daily rituals.
Eating, working, resting,
Then sleeping.
Boringly pointless.

Not so for Jesus people !
Believe in Him,
You'll find out !
Every day can be different.
Why ?
You've a new friend,
One that never leaves you.
You walk with Jesus,
You talk to Jesus.
You have new friends,
Friends who love Jesus.
All of you
Serving Jesus.
A Holy life !
Hallelujah !

TROUBLE MAKERS

Are you a trouble maker ?
If not, should you be ?
That sounds ominous !
Hold on though.
Jesus was a trouble maker !
The Jews thought so.
So much so
They killed Him.
His disciples also suffered.
So did Paul.
And countless Christians,
Through the ages,
And in this present day.
The reason ?
They stirred people up.
Told them God's teaching.
Preached and taught
For all to follow Jesus.
Even in churches
Those that are eager,
Those enthusiastic
Some call them trouble makers !

They have stirred things up
Brought life to sleepy churches.
They want people to work,
Work for Jesus,
To change their church,
Change it into being active.
Not always popular.
You can be a trouble maker !
Get on with it !
Following Jesus !
Be filled with fire,
Let no one dampen your spirits.
God comes first,
Always.
Remember though,
Do not aim to make trouble,
Just be dedicated,
Dedicated to put God first.
Keep at it,
Regardless.
God will bless your work.
Hallelujah !

TROUBLES ? THANK GOD !

Have you got troubles ?
Then thank the Lord !
You'll get help,
The best there is !
Thank Him for faith,
Believe in God's help.
Whatever the problem
Turn to your Lord.
God never sleeps,
He will hear your prayers
Day or night.
Be filled with thanks.
With faith-
You are on victory road.
Look back,
Look back on your life.
What happened to problems ?
Do you still have them ?

Have they gone away ?
Almost always,
They have gone !
Keep a record.
A prayer diary.
What did you ask,
What happened ?
Makes you aware,
Aware of what happened,
That God has helped.
Then testify !
Tell others what happened.
What God has done.
All of us -
We owe the Lord so much !
You are truly blessed.
Hallelujah !

TUG OF WAR

A contest of strength.
Heels dug in.
Hands gripping the rope.
Then the call.
The call to heave and heave.
Using all your strength,
Part of a team,
Minds and muscle
Working to win.
We enjoy being with a group.
There is good companionship,
But even so,
Each of us is unique.
All have different ideas.
Usually ideas to share.
Team work working.
Join a real team !

A Jesus Team.
All work as one,
All care for each other,
All love Jesus.
It's a together Team.
You'll learn joy,
The joy of Jesus people.
Dig in your heels,
Grip tight,
Pull against all odds
With all your mind.
Jesus Teams they win !
The best Teams anywhere !
Get on with it,
Never leave your Team.
Hallelujah !

TWO OR THREE

"Where there are two or three
I am there also",
So said Jesus.
It is so good to know,
It means everything !
So much can be done,
Done with a few people
For the Lord is there.
It just take two or three
Two or three to start a task,
A Godly task.
Small beginnings,
Yet growth can happen.
It can snowball.
It can be something great.

Believe in miracles,
God loves impossibilities.
You have a dream,
You have an idea ?
Something to advance His Kingdom ?
Tell your friends.
If they share the dream,
If they support the idea
Then all, pray hard.
Then move into action.
Keep your faith,
Go ahead,
Bring the Kingdom nearer,
God is with you.
Hallelujah !

UGLY AS SIN

Sin,
What could be uglier ?
Look at the media,
Give it their true name,
"Sinful News"!
It wallows,
In murders,
In immoral living,
In divorces,
Drunkenness,
Gossip,
Muggings and theft.
They love it,
It sells the papers.
Good news ?
It's hard to find !
The world lives in sin.
Ugliness everywhere.
Do not despair !
Be cheerful,
It's God's World,
He is in charge,
Just follow Him.

He is all powerful.
Recall,
It began with twelve disciples.
They, the twelve,
They spread good news,
Jesus taught them.
From just twelve,
Today millions and millions,
All following Christ !
A living miracle.
Every day decisions made,
Thousand coming to Jesus.
The media stays quiet.
Not their scene.
Goodness worldwide.
Where there are believers
There is goodness,
There is love,
There is Jesus.
Praise Him,
Belong from top to toe,
You love Him.
Hallelujah !

V.I.PS

What do you think ?
What are V.I.Ps ?
Royalty ?
Politicians ?
Film stars ?
Millionaires ?
None of those !
They are all temporary !
The solid truth :
You are the V.I.P !
The Very Important Person.
Each of you !
This is in God's eyes.
God loves you so much,
He sent Jesus His Son.
Read John 3.16.
He wants you,
He offers eternal life.
Jesus commanded,

"Tell others!".
You see
Those others,
They are V.I.Ps also !
God loves us all,
The big,
The small,
The fat, The thin,
The old and the young.
Marvellous
And all V.I.Ps.!
No exceptions.
Share the good news,
Go fishing,
Everyone is important.
Wanted by Jesus.
Keep on keeping on !
Hallelujah !

WANTED !

Wanted !
You !
You who do not believe.
Wanted !
All fence sitters.
Wanted for what ?
To know, to realise,
Jesus is Lord.
The Son of God.
Not just to know Him,
Not just to say "Yes",
But to solemnly promise,
Promise to serve Him,
Promise to be active,
To give your life,
Never to stop following Jesus.
Wanted !
All pew sitters !

That all must get up,
Be prepared to serve,
To show you love Him.
We all must be ready,
Ready to give
A cast iron commitment,
That is what is needed.
Think about dormant Christians,
If they come alive
A Christian revolution !
Thriving churches,
Solid revival.
Miracles !
Wake up the dormant !
Set them on fire !
Pray for this,
Then act upon it!
Hallelujah !

WASHING FEET

Jesus did this !
Would you ?
Off your own bat ?
Would you bathe beggars ?
Mother Theresa did !
Would you clean toilets,
Do other menial work ?
Nothing is menial
If you serve others.
Most of would be reluctant.
Jesus teaches limitless love.
We may say we love Jesus,
But do we love others ?
How much do we love Jesus ?
Real love for Him,
It breaks down all barriers.
Have your church try something !

Once a month go out,
Clean the road sides,
Clean up graffiti,
Find other menial tasks.
Actions are better than words.
But also tell of Jesus love.
A church showing Jesus !
Work such as this
It can bring miracles.
Christian examples
They can catch fish !
Pray about it !
If you do it
Expect results !
God is with you !
Hallelujah !

WEEKDAYS

What do you do,
Do on weekdays ?
Sunday you go to church,
Weekdays they can be weak days!
Spiritually weak days.
Every day,
Fill them spiritually.
Why do we stick just to Sundays !
It is wrong !
Monday onwards,
Every day belongs to God,
Belong to Godly days !
Especially Mondays,
No more Monday blues !
Thank God for every day.

Organise each day wth God.
Work out prayer times,
Work out your tasks.
Enlarge your day,
With Godly thoughts.
Talk to Him often.
Weekdays get better !
They seem more alive.
You are sharing each day with God.
You carry love into each day.
People will see the change !
Enjoy each day,
Share that enjoyment.
Hallelujah !

WHAT'S THIS BIBLE STUFF ?

Written so long ago
The Bible is still the best !
God's Word supreme.
God's own story.
His very words.
It's a compass,
It shows the way.
His Way.
The way to heaven,
To eternal life.
It saves lives,
Countless lives,
Millions and millions.
It gives you promises,
It teaches you love.
If you have never read The Bible
Turn to John's Gospel.
Read it slowly,
Write down John 3 verse 16.
Stop and ponder.
Say your first prayer !
That you believe.
Turn to Matthew Chapter 5,

Called the Sermon on the mount.
Wonderful words !
Caring words,
Loving words.
Go over it again,
Think quietly,
Take your time.
Pray again,
Simply,
In your own words.
For Christians,
Never, never stop reading.
Find the gems,
Underline them.
Finished The Bible ?
Nobody does !
Time to start again.
Time to find new things,
God's Word
It never ends,
The more you read
The more you will grow !
Hallelujah !

WHAT YOU WANNABEE ?

What are your aims ?
Worldly or heavenly ?
For most, worldly.
It's good to be successful.
Good to live comfortably.
Good to love your family,
To have many friends.
But this is not enough.
God put us on earth,
Too many ignore this.
People want this and that,
A one way route.
Even churchgoers,
Some can be self-centred.
We have to pause,
Give thought on our doings,
Which way are we going ?
Are we self-centred

Or are we God-centred ?
Probably some pruning needed !
Every Christian,
No exceptions,
God comes first.
Go God's way,
Switch off from self.
Travel from worldly to heavenly.
Get rid of worthless days.
Get rid of worthless ways.
Rid of selfishness.
No more Godless days.
Take the key to happiness,
Move to eternal life,
Be sure of it !
Worldly to heavenly,
What a difference !
Hallelujah !

WHERE ARE YOU ?

Where are you ?
It's a relevant question.
Think about it,
What stage in your life ?
What have you done ?
What so far ?
And what do you plan ?
Is your life worthwhile ?
Or is is worthless ?
Be honest !
Whatever you score
Go for a better score !
Face facts,
Real facts.
Where have you been ?
Where are you going ?
Going heavenwards
Or going towards hell ?
It's one or the other.

Which road are you on ?
Jesus repeatedly said,
"Follow me".
Are we doing this ?
Truthfully ?
Not just believing
But practical believing.
What have we done,
What are we doing
To serve our Saviour ?
Look at yourself !
Be fully alert,
Pull yourself together,
Kneel down,
Then move to serve.
Surveying is over,
All systems go
Going for Jesus.
Hallelujah !

WIMP OR WARRIOR ?

What is a wimp ?
He or she is weak willed.
No backbone.
Some Christians are wimps !
Those doing little or nothing.
And what is a warrior ?
One who battles for Christ.
Working with prayer,
Working with witness,
Working with love,
Always active.
Some churches are "wimpish",
How come ?
The leaders lack drive,
No enthusiasm,
No evangelism,
No efforts to plan ahead.
Too comfortable,
Almost stagnant.
The church that goes nowhere.

Wimps can change,
Change through to warriors !
One warrior can battle wimps !
Move in,
Arouse interest,
Instil movement.
One warrior can make the change,
Backed by God.
Enthusiasm is infectious,
The warrior can pass it on.
It can spread.
Wimps to warriors,
Just as God requires.
Wimpish churches,
Wimpish folk,
Potential warriors,
All of them.
Make them Godly,
The Lord will help.
Hallelujah !

YOU ARE RICH !

There are so many poor people,
Far more than those who are rich,
This in earthly terms.
And one thing is certain,
Riches will never last.
On the final day
The rich and the poor,
They are all equal.
Except for one thing !
Those who love Jesus,
Those born again,
Overnight they are rich !
Rich in joys,
Rich for ever,
They are with Jesus !
Not just for now,
Eternally !
Spiritual richness -
Aim for this now
There is nothing better.

The poorest of the poor
Can be a spiritual millionaire !
Richer than earthly tycoons.
Then some of the wealthy,
Some love the Lord,
They give funds readily,
They are good.
These are blessed,
They need not fear,
They travel the heavenly road.
Just remember,
Jesus was poor,
The disciples had no pay
Yet they were rich.
Count your blessing,
You have so many !
And more to come !
Life is rich with Jesus.
Keep with Him !
Hallelujah !

YOU COUNT !

There is no doubt,
You count.
Jesus loves you,
Always.
He knows you well,
Your good side
And your bad side
And He loves you.
You matter greatly.
You see,
He died for you.
For everyone.
He is so great
And he wants you,
He wants you on His team !
You count,

Will you respond ?
Give your heart and soul ?
Respond utterly ?
To the hilt ?
No two ways
In full or not at all.
Jesus wants dedication.
Simply,
Will you give your life ?
You count so much !
Decide right now,
Be on the Jesus Team,
Be born again,
You really count !
Hallelujah !

YOU MATTER

To God you matter.
If you do not believe
You still matter.
Matter greatly.
Just give it thought.
We know Jesus,
Jesus as Saviour.
Jesus was crucified,
He died to show God's love.
Love for the believers,
Love for the unbeliever.
You belong to God.
Believe it or not.
But realise this,
God wants you.
It is decision time.
God made you,
He gave you brains,
Use them !

Just think,
Jesus suffered for you,
Is that not enough ?
Does it not stir you ?
Don't hang about !
Jesus is calling,
Calling you by name.
Give Him your answer.
He wants to save your life,
To take you from the devil.
Sounds dramatic !
Believe it.
Two ways to go,
Only one good way.
Step onto God's highway,
Now !
You see,
You matter !
Hallelujah !

YOUR JESUS

We all have opinions.
They are bound to vary.
But what about Jesus ?
Be positive !
Be sure !
All should follow Jesus.
Jesus is very personal,
Personal to each of us.
Even so,
All should follow Him.
Belong to Jesus,
No holds barred.
Never never let go !
He is your Saviour,
Your personal Saviour,
Your companion,
Your friend,
Your everything.
Believe completely,

Know His love.
Don't just believe,
Be a disciple
Travel His road,
Serve him at all times,
Share your knowledge.
Share His love,
Share your desires,
Save lives for Jesus.
Be grateful,
A one hundred per cent follower.
Be sure He means everything,
There is nothing better !
Infect your friends,
Cast your nets,
Fill them
For Jesus' sake.
Hallelujah !

YOUR MOVE

Playing a game
You get your turn.
Your turn to move.
Life is more important.
There comes a time,
A time to make a move.
In life you can make two moves,
You have a choice.
Going the easy way,
The lazy way,
Or going the straight and narrow.
The Jesus Way
Or the devil's way.
Decisions may seem hard.
Unless you face reality.
That easy way,
That lazy way.
Why mention the devil,
Why think of hell !
Too may never use these words !
They figure often in The Bible.

They are real,
They are factual.
Jesus fought the devil.
So must we all.
The truth can be seen.
Act on what you understand.
Use your common sense !
The Jesus Way.
Your move,
Your move to win,
Win in life's game.
Meet up with jpoy,
Meet up with happiness,
Wonderful fellowship.
Most of all
Know you have eternal life.
Life with Jesus.
Rejoice !
Hallelujah !

YOUR PLAN

The plan for your life,
It is so important.
Be prepared for change.
Change it from your plan
Take God's plan.
His plan for you.
The Bible tells us,
We must follow God's plan.
Unique for you.
Your personal plan,
That is great !
It's wonderful !
Your own plan from God !
Especially for you !
You can call it "Your plan".
It puts you on the Jesus Team.

Without Him you are nothing,
With Him life is full.
Brimming over,
Joy and Happiness,
Expectation.
Full of purpose,
Ands God will direct you.
The plan will emerge,
Almost unknowingly,
It comes from the Lord.
Enjoy them,
Serve with eaagerness,
With love,
With Jesus !
Hallelujah !

YOUR SCORE

Score yourself !
Scores out of ten.
For each part of your life !
Be very honest,
Start your reckoning.
How much for your faith ?
How much for your prayer life ?
How much for service,
How much for real action ?
How much for love ?
Some are hard to score !
Why score ?
It's a kind of spring clean.
A real life check.

Seven or eight ?
Pretty good !
Anything lower need more work !
Whatever the score aim higher.
Know this though,
No one scores ten !
No one quite reaches perfection !
Work hard for Jesus,
Always,
Every day.
Do your very best,
God will know,
God will bless you !
Hallelujah !

100%

Following Jesus,
The are no "ifs",
There are no "buts".
Each Christian
Regardless of age,
Regardless of health,
All to score 100%
As close as possible !
Be close spiritually.
Your way to follow Jesus,
Anything else,
It just will not do !
Jesus showed His love,
Scored 100%.
Jesus showed dedication
Scored 100 %

Jesus obeyed His Father
Scored 100%.
He set the example,
We must follow.
Your worship and praise
Aim for 100%
Your actions,
Your service,
Your faith,
Your love
Your everything
Aim all for 100%
It's the Jesus way.
Follow it !
Hallelujah !

24/7 CHURCHES

Where are the churches,
Those that never shut ?
Every day,
All year long,
Always open ?
God's houses.
Not one in a thousand stay open.
Some open only on Sunday !
Then only in the morning.
Every church needs a prayer room.
A place well publicised,
For use for all,
No exceptions.
The place to go for help,
The rest room for the sad,
For the despairing,
For the lonely,
For those desperate.
A place to meet with God,
To have Christian love,
To be comforted,
To be reassured.
The Prayer Room,

Open every day,
For healthy churches
Open every night as well.
A place of refuge,
A place of succour,
Help one to one.
Impossible ?
Impracticable ?
Not so !
It is a great ministry.
Where there is a will
There is a way..
Let your town know
All may come.
All treated privately.
A spiritual rest room.
And it is positive !
It also leads people to church,
Leads them to believe.
Open a Prayer Room,
It's for every Church.
Do it with praise !
Hallelujah !

SNOWBALLING

Who scores full marks ?
Those who serve the Lord.
Serve him completely.
Those on fire,
Those who are contagious.
Revival in chapel or church,
It comes from such Christians.
It's like a snowball,
Running down a hill.
As it rolls
It gathers more snow,
It starts small,
It ends very big !
Those on fire,
They spread warmth to others,
They kindle fires,
Enthusiasm which spreads,
The Holy Spirit comes in.
Prayer meetings come in,
Inspired praying,

The Spirit moves within.
God takes charge.
From prayers to plans,
Plans to action,
All with God.
It's been done,
It is possible.
It needs just a small group,
It needs to gradually move,
Just like the snowball.
Picking up a few more.
Praying some more.
Getting warmer as they gather speed.
Moving with the Lord,
His will will triumph.
Revival is coming,
God wants this,
He plans it,
It will be done.
Hallelujah !